the **JESUS** SERIES

DID JESUS EXIST?

ARE THE RECORDS ABOUT HIM RELIABLE?

DON STEWART

TABLE OF CONTENTS

INTRODUCTION

This book looks at the question of the existence of Jesus Christ. Did Jesus exist? Was He a genuine historical figure? What records do we have that testify to His existence? Why should we trust what they say? What historical facts can we know for certain about the life and ministry of Jesus?

We will explore these and other important questions about the most influential person in history—Jesus of Nazareth.

QUESTION 1

Is It Important To Examine The Life Of Jesus Christ? What Makes Him So Special?

In this book we are going to look at the question of the existence of Jesus Christ, as well as the reliability of the written records about Him. In particular, we will examine the issue of the trustworthiness of the New Testament.

However, before we do this, there is a basic question that we need to answer. Why? Why is it so important to consider the life of Jesus Christ? Granted, He is a famous historical figure, but what makes Jesus so special? Why should we take the time to study who He was and what He did?

The reason that it is important to examine the life of Jesus of Nazareth goes beyond historical curiosity. When Jesus Christ came to earth, He claimed that the eternal destiny of every man, woman, and child would depend upon how they viewed Him.

If His claims are true, then the decision we make about Jesus will determine whether we spend eternity with Him, or without Him. Nothing could be more important.

Therefore, it is crucial that we understand where the life and ministry of Jesus fits into the total biblical story of God's dealings with the human race.

1. THE STORY OF THE BIBLE IS THE STORY OF GOD AND HUMANITY

The message of the Bible can be summed up as follows: In the beginning an all-powerful, personal God created the heavens and the earth. In His final act of creation, God created man and woman. The God of the Bible put them in a perfect environment giving them everything they needed for happiness.

But the man and woman sinned against God. Indeed, they disobeyed the only negative commandment which He had given them. Their disobedience led to a separation between them and God. They were banished from the paradise that God had provided for them.

2. GOD'S PROMISE TO THE HUMAN RACE: A SAVIOR

But God did not want matters to stay that way. He promised that He would take care of the sin that separated humanity from Himself. The Old Testament contains a number of promises that a Savior, or Messiah, would come and solve the sin problem.

The New Testament opens with the birth of this Promised One. His name is Jesus, which means "Yahweh is my salvation." He is also given the title "Christ," which means "the Messiah." He was the One whom the Old Testament prophets wrote and spoke about.

3. THE SAVIOR REVEALS HIMSELF TO THE WORLD

Some thirty years after Jesus' birth, a rugged individual named John the Baptist appeared in the Judean desert announcing the soon appearance of the promised Messiah. When Jesus arrived at the Jordan River where John was baptizing, He was identified by John as the "Lamb of God," the one who would take away the sins of the world.

After He was baptized, Jesus was tempted for forty days in the wilderness by the devil. Once His temptation was complete, the sinless Jesus began His public ministry.

4. JESUS' UNMATCHABLE DEEDS: HE DID THINGS NO ONE ELSE HAS EVER DONE

Jesus' public ministry lasted some three short years, but in that time He lived a life such as no one has lived before or since. He did things that no one else has ever done. He healed the lame, the blind, the deaf and the mute.

On one occasion Jesus caused a storm to immediately cease. His friend Lazarus was four days dead but Jesus brought him back to life. The people of His day, upon seeing the miracles that Jesus did, testified, "We never saw anything like this!" (Mark 2:12). Indeed, nobody else has ever seen such things.

5. JESUS' UNMATCHABLE WORDS: HE SAID THINGS NO ONE ELSE HAS EVER SAID

Jesus also said things such as no one else has ever said. After He finished delivering the Sermon on the Mount to the people, which is recorded in Matthew 5-7, the Scripture records that the crowds were astonished at His teaching. He spoke to them as One who had authority.

Indeed, Jesus claimed authority. He had authority over disease, authority over nature, authority over the supernatural, and authority over life and death. He claimed to be the One who had the power to forgive sins, to raise the dead on judgment day, and to grant eternal life to whoever believed in Him.

6. JESUS DIED FOR THE WORLD'S SINS AND THEN ROSE FROM THE DEAD

He was betrayed by one of His own disciples and crucified under the Roman governor, Pontius Pilate. Yet the New Testament records that three days after His death He appeared to His disciple alive! He had risen from the dead just as He said He would. By doing this, Jesus demonstrated the truth of His claims.

Furthermore, the Bible says Jesus' death on the cross was for the sins of the world. His death has made it possible for humankind to have their broken relationship with God restored. To receive forgiveness of sin, and life everlasting life, Scripture says that one must believe in Jesus Christ. This means accepting His sacrifice on our behalf.

Eternal life is thus a free gift. We cannot earn it. All we can do is believe in Him—for Jesus Christ has done it all.

7. JESUS ASCENDED INTO HEAVEN AND HAS PROMISED TO RETURN

The Bible also says that Jesus ascended into heaven some forty days after His resurrection. He has been exalted at the right hand of God. Scripture promises that He will return someday and judge the living and the dead.

8. OUR VIEW OF JESUS DETERMINES WHERE WE WILL SPEND ETERNITY

Finally, according to Scripture, what we do with Jesus Christ will determine where we spend eternity. Humanity is divided into two groups— the saved and the lost. Those who believe in Jesus, the saved, will enjoy everlasting life in His presence. Those who do not believe in Him are the lost. They will spend eternity apart from God because they have rejected the only means of salvation which God has provided.

This briefly sums up the message of Scripture. As we can see, the stakes could not be higher. If Jesus is the One whom He claimed to be, then the eternal destiny of each of us is based upon what we do with Him. Therefore, it is crucial that we examine the life and ministry of Jesus Christ to discover if His claims are true.

However, before we can do this, we must look at some preliminary questions. Did Jesus really exist? Are the records about Him reliable? In other words, can we trust what the New Testament says about what He said and what He did?

SUMMARY TO QUESTION 1
IS IT IMPORTANT TO EXAMINE THE LIFE OF JESUS?

It is crucial that each of us take the time to examine the life and ministry of Jesus Christ. Why? It is because Jesus Christ's identity is of utmost importance. It is imperative that we consider the claims made about Him and see if He is indeed the One whom He made Himself out to be. We can make the following observations.

To begin with, the story of the Bible is the story of the human race. It tells us who we are, how we got here, that there is a God who exists, as well as what He requires of us. From Scripture, we find that a perfect God created a perfect world. However, this perfection was spoiled when the first humans, Adam and Eve, rebelled against God. Their sin caused separation from God.

Immediately the Lord promised humanity that He would someday provide a Savior who would heal the broken relationship between God and the human race. Some two thousand years ago this promise was realized when, in the fullness of time, God the Son, Jesus Christ, came into our world.

The four gospels record the life and ministry of Jesus. We find that He said things which nobody else has ever said, and did things which nobody else has ever done. Jesus Christ was unique.

Indeed, He was one-of-a-kind, having no like or equal. Among other things, Jesus claimed to be the one way in which a person could reach the one God. There would be no salvation apart from Him.

The gospels tell us that Jesus died on a cross for the sins of the world—the innocent dying for the guilty. However, He did not stay dead. Three days later He rose from the dead. His resurrection demonstrated that the claims which He made about Himself were true.

Forty days after His resurrection Jesus ascended into heaven. He remains at the right hand of God waiting the time He will return. When He does return He will judge the living and the dead.

The Bible says that our view of Jesus Christ will determine where we will spend eternity. Those who trust Him as Savior will receive everlasting life, while those who reject His free gift of salvation will spend eternity apart from Him.

If His claims are true, then there is no issue which is of greater significance for the human race. Consequently, it is exceedingly important that we examine the life and ministry of Jesus Christ.

Yet, before we can consider what the New Testament says about Jesus, we must answer some preliminary questions about His existence as well as the reliability of the records that chronicle His life and ministry. The rest of this book will do just that.

How Do We Know That A Person Named Jesus Of Nazareth Truly Existed? Could He Be A Myth?

Did a person named Jesus of Nazareth exist? Could Jesus actually have been a mythical person? Perhaps the stories about Him were all made-up. What is the historical evidence that Jesus Christ truly existed?

Before we can answer questions about His identity, we must first establish the fact of His existence. This is not difficult to do, for both friend and foe alike testify that the man, Jesus, did indeed exist. The evidence is as follows.

WE HAVE A FIRSTHAND SOURCE TO HIS EXISTENCE: THE NEW TESTAMENT

The only firsthand source that we have of the life and ministry of Jesus is found in the New Testament. The New Testament consists of twenty-seven separate documents that were written by people living in the first century who had personal contact with Jesus.

All of these writings testify to the existence of Jesus Christ. These New Testament witnesses can be divided as follows: the Four Gospels, the Book of Acts, the Letters of Paul, and the writings of other disciples.

1. THE TESTIMONY OF THE FOUR GOSPELS

The four gospels, Matthew, Mark, Luke and John, each give an account of the life of Jesus. Matthew and John were two of Jesus' twelve disciples. They wrote with firsthand knowledge of what Jesus said and did.

Mark wrote about the life of Jesus from the viewpoint of Simon Peter—also one of the twelve. In fact, Marks' gospel maybe be a word-for-word report of what Peter said. Luke's account was based upon the testimony of eyewitnesses.

The four gospels chronicle the ministry of Jesus in a historical setting. Luke, for example, provides the names of the rulers living at the time when John the Baptist, Jesus' forerunner, appeared. He wrote.

> In the fifteenth year of the reign of Tiberius Caesar—when Pontius Pilate was governor of Judea, Herod tetrarch of Galilee, his brother Philip tetrarch of Iturea and Traconitis, and Lysanias tetrarch of Abilene—during the high priesthood of Annas and Caiaphas, the word of God came to John son of Zechariah in the desert (Luke 3:1,2 NIV).

Note the fact that there are seven specific historical reference points in these two verses. Among other things, Luke tells us who the reigning Caesar was at the time of Jesus, who governed Judea, as well as the names of the current High Priest's in Israel.

The detailed historical nature of his account is clear. The same holds true for the other gospels.

Therefore, we have four independent writings, each of them recording specific eyewitness testimony to the fact that Jesus did exist. This puts the existence of Jesus Christ beyond all reasonable doubt.

2. THE TESTIMONY OF THE BOOK OF ACTS

There is more evidence. The Book of Acts, written by Luke, records the birth and rise of the New Testament church. After Jesus came back from the dead, He gave His disciples instructions on how to proclaim His message to the world. The Book of Acts records the struggles of His disciples to accomplish this task. Their experiences and preaching give further testimony to Jesus' existence.

3. THE WRITINGS OF THE APOSTLE PAUL

The letters of Paul make up a large part of the New Testament. Paul, formerly named Saul, was a devout Jew who hated Christians to the point that he put them in jail and consented to their execution.

Yet one day, when he was on the road to Damascus to persecute Christians, the risen Jesus appeared to him. This resulted in Saul's conversion to the Apostle Paul. The remainder of his life was spent spreading the good news of Jesus Christ. Paul's letters give convincing testimony to Jesus' existence.

Paul is an important witness to Jesus since he corroborates what is taught in the four gospels. From Paul, we learn that Jesus was Jewish, a descendant of King David, and was the promised Messiah. The Apostle Paul also taught that Jesus' horrible death of crucifixion was for the purpose of taking upon Himself the penalty for the sins of the world.

Paul, like the gospel writers, tells us that Jesus rose from the dead the third day. Paul relates that Jesus was seen alive by many people after His death. This includes James, His own brother, who previously had not believed in Him.

Paul also tells us that Jesus was worshipped as God by the first Christians. This is very important to note. The idea of the deity of Christ was not something that the later church invented as stories about Him began to circulate. From the very beginning, it was recognized that Jesus was a human being but that He was also more than a human being.

4. THE WRITINGS OF OTHER DISCIPLES

The remainder of the New Testament consists of letters by certain disciples of Jesus. We have two from Simon Peter (1 and 2 Peter), one from James, one from Jude, four from John (1,2,3 John and the Book of Revelation) and the anonymous letter to the Hebrews.

These writings contain instruction and encouragement to the believers in Jesus Christ. They give firsthand testimony to the fact of Jesus' life and ministry, as well as confirming the account of Jesus as found in the four gospels.

The Book of James is of particular interest because he is identified as the brother of Jesus. As we mentioned, according to John's gospel, James, as well as Jesus' other brothers, did not believe in Him during His earthly ministry. James became a believer in Christ sometime after Jesus' crucifixion. Thus, his testimony is like that of Saul of Tarsus—it is that of an unbeliever who became a believer after the resurrection of Christ.

VERY FEW SCHOLARS DOUBT JESUS' EXISTENCE

While at one time it was fashionable to doubt the existence of Jesus of Nazareth, the situation has changed today. Few, if any, scholars would attempt to deny Jesus' existence. There is too much reliable evidence from the New Testament, as well as from other sources, that show He was a genuine historical character.

Most unbelieving scholars attempt to put it this way: While Jesus did exist, we cannot really know that much about Him. However, as we will see, this is simply not true.

As we look into the evidence for Jesus' existence, and the reliability of the records about Him, we will find every reason to believe that we have accurate first-hand information about His life and ministry. This account is found in the New Testament.

SUMMARY TO QUESTION 2
HOW DO WE KNOW THAT JESUS EXISTED?

There is really no doubt that a man named Jesus of Nazareth existed. Both friend and foe testify to that fact. Indeed, we have twenty-seven different New Testament documents which unanimously bear witness to Jesus' existence.

First, we have the four gospels. They record the highlights of the life and ministry of Jesus. Two of the writers, Matthew and John, were eyewitnesses. Mark took down the words of another eyewitness, Simon Peter.

Luke's gospel consisted of interviewing those who knew Jesus intimately. Given the fact of the numerous historical reference points we find in the gospels, as well as specific details of Jesus' ministry, the fact of His existence should not be an issue.

However, there is more. The Book of Acts chronicles the history of the early church as it started from Jerusalem and moved on to Rome. Acts begins with Jesus giving instruction to His followers. The sermons recorded in Acts continually testify to Jesus' existence, as well as His miraculous deeds.

A third source comes from the Apostle Paul. He was an unbeliever during Jesus' earthly ministry. As a persecutor of believers, Saul of Tarsus became a believer in Jesus as he met the risen Lord on the road to Damascus. He gives further corroboration that Jesus of Nazareth existed.

Finally, there are other New Testament writers, James, John, Peter, Jude and the anonymous writer to the Hebrews. Each of these independent sources provides additional testimony that Jesus truly lived.

Thus, it is difficult, if not impossible, in our day to attempt to deny His existence. We will discover that the evidence shows that not only did Jesus exist, the records that we have about Him in the four gospels presents a reliable testimony to His life and ministry.

QUESTION 3

What Do Early Jewish Writings, Such As Those Of Flavius Josephus, Say About Jesus? (Extra-biblical Jewish Evidence)

The twenty-seven separate documents of the New Testament testify to Jesus' existence as well as providing information about His public ministry. But what about other evidence that exists? Apart from the New Testament what information do we find about Jesus? What do other sources tell us? In this question, we will look at what the Jewish sources have to say.

THE EARLY JEWISH SOURCES

There is some evidence for Jesus' existence that can be found in early Jewish sources. They include the writings of first-century historian Flavius Josephus, a man named Rabbi Eliezer, and the Jewish writings known as the Talmud.

1. THE TESTIMONY OF FLAVIUS JOSEPHUS (A.D. 37-100)

Apart from the New Testament, the earliest testimony of Jesus, that has survived to this day, is from the Jewish writer Flavius Josephus. His work is of tremendous value as he had a unique vantage point to record the political and religious events of the times. It has also been determined that he was an accurate historian.

Josephus was born around the year A.D. 37 in the city of Jerusalem. He became a leader of a movement in Galilee that rebelled against Rome. On one occasion, during the siege of Jotapata (Yodfat), he and his men were completely surrounded by the Roman army. They decided, by unanimous vote, to commit suicide. Josephus was to be the last to take his own life.

Instead, he gave himself up to the Romans after all of his men had killed themselves. He gained the favor of the Emperor Vespasian, as well as his son Titus, by agreeing to persuade the Jews to give up their revolt against Rome. He was soon seen as a traitor against his own country.

Despite his lack of personal integrity, Josephus has left us with a number of written works. They include two major works known as "Jewish History," or "Antiquities of the Jews" and "Wars of the Jews."

These two works comprise 1,800 pages. "Wars of the Jews," or *Bellum Judaicum* as it called is in Latin, is an account of the Jewish wars from the time of Antiochus IV, 170 B.C, until the destruction of Jerusalem in A.D. 70. The work was published in A.D. 77.

Antiquitates Judaicae, as it is called in Latin, or "Jewish History," or "Antiquities," was published in A.D. 93. It presents the history of the Jews from the creation of the world until the time of Josephus.

He also wrote a work called *Contra Apion*, "Against Apion." This was an answer to a Jewish skeptic named Apion. Josephus also wrote as his own autobiography.

In his writings, Josephus describes a number of characters that are also mentioned in the New Testament. They include: Pontius Pilate, Quirinius, Archelaus, James the brother of Jesus, John the Baptist, and Jesus Himself.

JOSEPHUS' REFERENCE TO JAMES

In his "Antiquities of the Jews," Josephus has a reference to James, the brother of Jesus. It reads as follows.

> He convened a meeting of the Sanhedrin and brought before them a man named James, the brother of Jesus, who was called the Christ, and certain others. He accused them of having transgressed the law and delivered them up to be stoned.

The trustworthiness of this passage is not in dispute. In it, we find the confirmation that Jesus had a brother named James as well as the fact that some people believed Jesus to be the Messiah.

THE PASSAGES IN THE WRITINGS OF JOSEPHUS THAT REFER TO JESUS

Our main interest in the writings of Josephus concerns what we find in his *Antiquities of the Jews*. In book eighteen, subparagraph three, it reads as follows.

> Now there was about this time, Jesus, a wise man, if it be lawful to call him a man, for he was a doer of wonderful works—a teacher of such men as receive the truth with pleasure. He drew over to him both many of the Jews, and many of the Gentiles.

> He was the Christ; and when Pilate, at the suggestion of the principal men amongst us, had condemned him to the cross, those who loved him at first did not forsake him, for he appeared to them alive again the third day, as the divine prophets had foretold these and ten thousand other wonderful things concerning him; and the tribe of Christians, so named from him, are not extinct at this day (*Antiquities*, XVIII, III).

This passage is known as the *Testimonium Flavium*. The complete trust-worthiness of this passage has been called into question for a number of reasons.

THE VARIOUS VIEWS OF JOSEPHUS' TESTIMONY

Basically, these statements of Josephus concerning Jesus have been treated in three different ways by scholars. We can briefly summarize them as follows.

OPTION 1: THE ENTIRE PASSAGE WAS BELIEVED TO BE ADDED LATER BY CHRISTIANS

Some believe the entire passage has been written by later Christians. This makes it unauthentic and of no worth as an independent source for the life of Jesus.

OPTION 2: THE ENTIRE PASSAGE WAS WRITTEN BY JOSEPHUS

Others believe the entire passage, as it now stands, was written by Josephus. This would make it a valuable testimony to Jesus' existence.

OPTION 3: PART OF THE PASSAGE IS AUTHENTIC AND PART WAS ADDED LATER

A third point of view believes that the passage contains some authentic material about Jesus, as well as, some later additions by Christians.

REASONS FOR ACCEPTING JOSEPHUS' AS VALID

There are a number of reasons for accepting Josephus' testimony, as it now stands, as valid. They are as follows.

1. The Greek text is characteristic of the way Josephus wrote. The present form of the text fits with everything else that came from him.

2. The fourth century historian, Eusebius, knew the passage in this form and accepted it as historical. Furthermore, Eusebius is an excellent witness to events in church history.

3. Other church fathers, such as Jerome and Ambrosius, also accepted the form of this passage as coming from Josephus. This gives further testimony to its authenticity.

4. The phrases used in this passage, are typically Jewish. Indeed, they are not what we would expect from later Gentiles Christians.

REASONS FOR REJECTING ALL OR PART OF THE PASSAGE

There are a number of reasons given as to why certain parts of the passage, or the entire passage, is believed to have been added later by Christians.

Specifically, there are three questionable parts to the statement of Josephus which some believe show that he could not have written it. They are as follows.

First, there is the statement, "if it is lawful to call him a man." This seems to indicate Josephus believed Jesus was more than a mere human. It is contended the Jewish Josephus would never have written something like this. Since he did not believe Jesus to be the divine Son of God, he probably would not have referred to Him in this manner.

In addition, in this passage, Josephus referred to Jesus as the Messiah, or the Christ. In the earlier passage, which he wrote about James, Jesus' brother, Josephus refers to Jesus as "the so-called Christ." He realized that others believed Jesus to be the Christ but he himself did not believe this.

Third, in this passage, Josephus says that Jesus rose from the dead. It is not likely Josephus would claim that Jesus had been raised from the dead.

In addition, it has been argued that the church Father Origen did not know the text in its present form. He cites the passage but not in the same form as we have it today. This has led to the theory that the passage was added sometime after he lived.

There is something else. The writings of Josephus were copied by "Christian" copyists. This would increase the possibility that the text may have been added to somewhere down the line to portray Jesus in a more favorable light.

THEY ARE NOT NECESSARILY UNSOLVABLE PROBLEMS

To some, these three portions in the testimony of Josephus are not necessarily unsolvable. The usual responses are along this line.

The phrase, "if it is lawful to call him a man" may not be Josephus' statement that Jesus was divine. Since he had earlier referred to Jesus as the so-called Christ, this reference may be understood in that light.

It is also possible that this statement was later added by Christians. However, this does not take away from the fact that the basic trustworthiness of this passage seems to be established.

The concept of the Messiah among the Jews at that time was not always clear. Josephus, for example, also understood Vespasian as fulfilling the office of the Messiah. Josephus may have accepted Jesus to be the Messiah, in some sense, without being a believer in Him in the New Testament sense of the term. Again, it is possible that this statement was added by later Christians.

Furthermore, what Josephus said about the resurrection may only be an indication of what he knew Jesus' followers believed about Him. Indeed, it not necessarily what he believed, or what he thought was true.

The fact that Christians were responsible for copying the text of Josephus does not necessarily mean they added to what he wrote, or invented the entire passage. Indeed, the description of Jesus in Josephus is very Jewish—it is not how later Gentile Christians would describe Jesus.

THE PASSAGE BELONGS IN THE WRITINGS OF JOSEPHUS

Whether or not the entire passage is genuine, there is strong evidence that it belongs in the writings of Josephus.

WHAT WE LEARN FROM JOSEPHUS ABOUT JESUS

There seems to be no good reason to dismiss the entire account of Josephus as unauthentic. In fact, a good case can still be made for accepting the entire passage as authentic. This being the case, the following historical facts can be derived from Josephus' statement.

1. Jesus of Nazareth existed.

2. Some people believed Him to be the Messiah.

3. He had many disciples from both Jews and Gentiles.

4. He was condemned to death by crucifixion under Pontius Pilate.

5. His disciples testified that Jesus rose from the dead three days after His death.

6. His disciples proclaimed the resurrection of Christ.

7. Many Christians existed at the time Josephus' wrote.

Josephus, therefore, adds corroborating testimony to Jesus. While not a contemporary, he lived and wrote about sixty years after the events of Jesus' ministry. Thus, his information is valuable because it confirms the basic outline of New Testament events.

Furthermore, we have discovered that Josephus has generally proven to be an accurate historian on other matters which he wrote about. This being the case, his reference to Jesus, whether or not entirely authentic, is a valuable early testimony.

THE ARABIC TEXT OF JOSEPHUS' STATEMENT ABOUT JESUS

The text of Josephus' various works have been transmitted to us in Greek. However, in 1972, an Arabic text of Josephus was discovered and translated. What is of interest to us is that the section than mentions Jesus is slightly different in the Arabic version than in the Greek version.

There are a number of scholars who believe this text is closer to what Josephus originally wrote. It still testifies to Jesus' existence without acknowledging Him as the Messiah. Whatever, the case may eventually be, Jesus' existence is confirmed, as well as a number of important details about Him, by the writings of this first-century Jewish writer.

2. RABBI ELIEZER (AROUND A.D. 90)

A second possible early Jewish testimony to Jesus is from a man named Rabbi Eliezer. Eliezer is believed to have written the following in the last decade of the first century. We read the following description of what he said.

> Rabbi Eliezer said, Balaam looked forth and saw that there was a man, born of woman, who should rise up and seek to make himself God, and to cause the whole world to go astray. Therefore, God gave the power to the voice of Balaam that all the peoples of the world might hear, and thus he spoke. Give heed that you go not astray after that man; for it is written, God is not man that he should lie. And if he says that he is God he is a liar, and he will deceive and say that he departed and comes again at the end. He says and he shall not perform.

Though Rabbi Eliezer does not name the person under consideration, it is obviously Jesus. Balaam was one of the derogatory terms used for Jesus in early Jewish writings. The traditional Jewish explanation of Jesus is one who led people astray.

This text confirms the claims of the New Testament that Jesus was God Himself. It also corroborates Jesus promise that He would come again. Therefore, from a hostile source, we have confirming evidence about certain aspects of Jesus' life and ministry.

3. THE TALMUD

The Talmud is a collection of Jewish writings constituting their religious and civil law. They were completed by A.D. 500. The Talmud contains references to Jesus. They are as follows.

> On the eve of Passover they hanged Yeshu (of Nazareth) and the herald went before him for forty days saying (Yeshu of Nazareth) is going to be stoned in that he has practiced sorcery and beguiled and led astray Israel. Let everyone know aught in his defense come and plead for him. But they found naught in his defense and hanged him on the eve of Passover (*The Babylonian Talmud, Sanhedrin* 43a, "Eve of Passover").

This reference about Jesus is looked at two different ways among scholars.

Some see it to be suspect. For one thing, the reference to Jesus is late—it is not from an early source. There are a number of things about it that are historically suspect. The idea that Jesus was going to be stoned to death is not historical. Neither is the idea that there were forty days in which people could come forward in His defense. This passage does contain the conventional Jewish explanation that Jesus practiced sorcery.

In addition, it says that Jesus was hanged. While this could possible be a reference to Jesus' crucifixion, hanging on a tree, some believe it refers to another type of death. Whatever the case may be, this reference is too late to be of any help in independently confirming Jesus' existence.

However, others see this text as corroborating a number of facts about Jesus. The gospels do say that people attempted to stone Jesus on certain occasions.

The idea that a herald went out for forty days to testify to the charges against Jesus and look for witnesses to come to His defense is not found in the New Testament. In fact, the only witnesses that were looked for at Jesus' trial were false witnesses!

Hanging is indeed seen as synonymous with crucifixion.

This reference also corroborates the New Testament picture of how unbelievers viewed Jesus. They accused Him of being demon-possessed. We read of this in Matthew.

> But when the Pharisees heard about the miracle, they said, "No wonder he can cast out demons. He gets his power from Satan, the prince of demons" (Matthew 12:24 NLT).

This reference also confirms that Jesus death took place at the time of the Passover.

What we can conclude about this reference, though admittedly later in history, is that the charges against Jesus are consistent with what other sources tell us.

The Talmud contains a further reference to Jesus which says Jesus was born out of wedlock. This is also consistent with the attitude toward Jesus found in the New Testament. The Jewish religious leaders accused Him of being an illegitimate child. Jesus said.

> No, you are obeying your real father when you act that way. They replied, "We were not born out of wedlock! Our true Father is God himself" (John 8:41 NLT).

We know that there was continuing controversy over Jesus' parentage. An ancient testimony attempts to make Jesus' actual father a Roman soldier by the name of Panthera.

While both of these references contain information that is, in some ways, consistent with the New Testament account of how the Jewish leaders viewed Jesus, they are too late in history to be of any real historical worth.

THE JEWS DID NOT GIVE MANY DETAILS ABOUT FALSE TEACHERS

It should be noted that the ancient Jewish writings did not go into any extensive detail about any of the teachers they considered to be false. It was not their purpose, or their desire, to write very much about those whom they considered to be blasphemers or liars. Therefore, we should not expect to find many references in their writings about Jesus.

THERE IS SOME INDEPENDENT CONFIRMATION OF JESUS

Consequently, from the Jewish evidence we now possess, there is relatively little independent information that can establish anything certain about Him.

What little it does tell us corroborates the New Testament claim that Jesus was a teacher who had certain disciples that followed Him. In His ministry, He healed the sick, worked miracles, and cast out demons. It also confirms that from the beginning, the Jewish leadership considered Jesus to be a false teacher and a deceiver of the people.

All of these facts further substantiate the New Testament account of Jesus.

SUMMARY TO QUESTION 3
WHAT DO EARLY JEWISH WRITINGS, SUCH AS THOSE OF FLAVIUS JOSEPHUS, SAY ABOUT JESUS? (EXTRA-BIBLICAL JEWISH SOURCES)

There is no written testimony to the life and ministry of Jesus of Nazareth in Jewish sources that were contemporary with Him. At least, nothing written has survived. The sources we do have are later in time.

The earliest and most helpful source is that of first-century writer Flavius Josephus. He mentions a number of facts about Jesus which are consistent with the things that are recorded in the New Testament.

For example, from Josephus we learn that Jesus of Nazareth existed. Furthermore, there were some people who believed Him to be the promised Messiah. Josephus wrote that Jesus had many disciples from both Jews and Gentiles.

We also find that Jesus was condemned to death by crucifixion under Pontius Pilate but His disciples testified that Jesus rose from the dead three days after His death. In addition, Josephus said His disciples proclaimed the resurrection of Christ. Many Christians existed at the time Josephus' wrote. These facts are consistent with the New Testament account of Jesus.

While the passage found in Josephus' writings about Jesus is in dispute, there are still good reasons to believe that some, if not all of it, is valid.

The later Jewish references are of no independent historical worth. They continue promoting the idea that Jesus was a sorcerer who practiced magic, as well as one who had an illegitimate birth. They attempted to make Him out as a deceiver and blasphemer, and by doing so, admitted that He existed. This description is consistent with how unbelievers viewed Him.

What we can conclude from these writings is that they confirm some of the basic facts of the New Testament account of the life and ministry of Jesus from how hostile Jewish sources would look at Him.

What Do Early, Non Jewish, Writings Tell Us About Jesus? (Extra-biblical Gentile Sources)

There are no first-hand Jewisu

h sources from the time of Jesus Christ that adds to our knowledge of His life and ministry. But what about non-Jewish sources? Do the writings of Greeks and Romans give us any information about Jesus? What do they tell us?

THERE IS NO FIRSTHAND INFORMATION FROM GREEK AND ROMAN SOURCES

The situation is basically the same with the Greek and Roman writers. We have no firsthand information about the life and ministry of Jesus that was written by His contemporaries. However, we do have a few later sources that give us some information. We can list them as follows.

THALLUS (C. A.D. 52)

The earliest non-Jewish source about Jesus comes from a man named Thallus. Although the identification of his nationality has been disputed, it seems that Thallus was a Samaritan historian. In other words, he was half-Jew, half-Gentile. Unfortunately, his writings have not survived to the present day.

Another writer, however Julius Africanus, who wrote about A.D. 221, cites the writings of Thallus. According to Africanus, Thallus attempted to write a history of the eastern Mediterranean world from the time of the Trojan War.

Africanus informs us that Thallus attempted to explain away the three-hour period of darkness at the time of Christ's crucifixion. He wrote.

> Thallus, in the third book of his histories, explains away this darkness as an eclipse of the sun—unreasonable, as it seems to me.

In attempting to explain the three-hour period of darkness when Christ was upon the cross, Thallus gives testimony that such an event did occur. His non-supernatural explanation of the event is impossible because Christ died at the time of Passover when there was a full moon and a solar eclipse cannot take place at the time of a full moon. We are indebted to Julius Africanus for this glimpse into the writings of Thallus.

THALLUS IS CONFIRMED BY TERTULLIAN

The corroboration of Thallus, that there was an unnatural darkness at the crucifixion of Christ, seems to have further confirmation from other ancient sources. The church father Tertullian, writing in the second century, testified that the darkness was not limited to Palestine but was also seen throughout the entire Roman Empire.

THE TESTIMONY OF PHLEGON

There is more. An ancient Greek writer named Phlegon wrote a chronology around the year A.D. 137. One of the things he reported was a great eclipse of the sun during the fourth year of the 202nd Olympiad. This would correspond to A.D. 33. He said that it became night during the sixth hour of the day, or noon. The event was so profound that some sort of explanation seemed necessary. Yet, this could not have been a solar eclipse, if it occurred during the time of the Passover, when the moon was full.

THE LETTER OF MARA BAR-SERAPION (AFTER A.D. 73)

In the British Museum, there is a letter that was written sometime during the first century A.D. by a father to his son who found himself in prison. In this letter, the father compares the death of Socrates, Pythagoras and a wise king. He wrote the following.

> What advantage did the Jews gain from executing their wise King? It was just after that their kingdom was abolished. . . But Socrates did not die for good; he lived on in the teaching of Plato. Pythagoras did not die for good; he lived on in the statue of Hera. Nor did the wise King die for good; he lived on in the teaching which he had given.

It is very probable the wise king referred to was Jesus. The writer mentions the Jews lost their kingdom soon after they executed their wise king. Less than forty years after the crucifixion of Jesus, the Romans destroyed the city of Jerusalem and the Jews were scattered from their land. If this is the case, then we have an independent testimony to Jesus' existence from the late first century A.D.

CORNELIUS TACITUS (EARLY SECOND CENTURY)

Cornelius Tacitus, a Roman historian living in the early second century, wrote about the reign of Caesar Nero. Tacitus records that Nero shifted the blame for the burning of Rome from himself to the Christians.

> Hence to suppress the rumor, he falsely charged with guilt, and punished with the most exquisite tortures, the persons commonly called Christians, who were hated for their enormities. Christus, the founder of the name was put to death by Pontius Pilate, procurator of Judea in the reign of Tiberius: not only through Judea, where the mischief originated, but through the city of Rome also (Annals, XV, 44).

Tacitus also refers to Christianity in another section of his Histories when speaking of the burning of the temple. We know about this reference from another writer, Sulpicius Serverus (Chronicles, 30.6), who preserved the reference from Tacitus.

TACITUS WRITINGS CONFIRM DETAILS FOUND IN THE NEW TESTAMENT

Tacitus' writings confirm the existence of Jesus Christ as well as the spread of Christianity at an early date. Several other details that he mentions line up with the New Testament. They can be listed as follows.

1. Christ's public ministry began during the reign of Tiberius Caesar (Luke 3:1).

2. Pontius Pilate was governor of Judea at the time of Christ's death (Matthew 27:6).

3. Jesus was put to death as a criminal (Luke 23:2).

4. His death occurred in Judea (Mark 11:6).

5. Jesus' death stopped the "superstition" for a short time but it soon broke out again.

Again, we have non-biblical testimony that supports the New Testament record. The statement of Tacitus, that the "superstition had been checked for the moment, but then broke out again," has been seen by some commentators as a reference to Jesus' resurrection. However, not all scholars agree with this interpretation of Tacitus' statement.

Tacitus, in his mention of Christianity, confirms an important point about the religion of Jesus—it was based upon a person who had been executed by the orders of Pontius Pilate.

Thus, the question arises, "Why would so many people worship a man who had suffered the death of a criminal?" The Christian answer is something that Tacitus did not record—they believe that Jesus rose from the dead. The belief of Christians, that Jesus rose from the dead, accounts for their zeal to spread the message to everyone. Otherwise, there would be no point in worshipping Him.

Tacitus also confirms that Christians were willing to die for their belief in Christ. Again, one may properly ask the question, "Why would one die for an executed religious leader?"

There is something else at issue here. Some have questioned where Tacitus derived his information about Jesus and the early Christians. Was it something he independently verified, or was he merely repeating what the Christians were saying about Jesus? Though some try to accuse Tacitus of merely repeating the words of Christians, there are good reasons to believe Tacitus could independently verify what he knew of Christians and Christ.

PLINY THE YOUNGER (C. A.D. 112)

Pliny the Younger was governor of Bithynia. He wrote a letter to the Emperor Trajan saying that he had killed numerous Christians. He also had this to say of the Christians.

> They were in the habit of meeting on a certain fixed day before it was light, when they sang in alternate verse a hymn to Christ as to a god, and bound themselves to the solemn oath, not to do any wicked deeds, and never to deny a truth when they should be called upon to deliver it up (Epistles, X, 96).

Pliny confirms the historical accuracy of some of the details of the New Testament.

1. He says the Christians met on a fixed day (Acts 20:7).

2. Pliny noted that the Christians prayed to Jesus as God. Some translations read, "chanting as if to a god."

Consequently, we have early testimony from a non-Christian source that Christians met on a regular basis and worshipped Christ as God.

SUETONIUS (C. A.D. 120)

Suetonius was a court official under the Emperor Hadrian. He wrote of Claudius Caesar. In his writings, we find the following statement.

> As the Jews were making constant disturbances at the instigation of Chestus he expelled them from Rome (*Life of Claudius*, 25.4).

The fact that the Jews were expelled from Rome by Claudius is also recorded in Scripture. We read about this in the Book of Acts.

> There he became acquainted with a Jew named Aquila, born in Pontus, who had recently arrived from Italy with his wife, Priscilla. They had been expelled from Italy as a result of Claudius Caesar's order to deport all Jews from Rome (Acts 18:2 NLT).

This would have included the Jewish Christians. At that early time in the history of the church, there was no distinction made between them and other Jews who had not believed in Jesus.

There is some question as to whether the term "Chestus" refers to Jesus. Some have argued that it refers to an actual Jewish person who was in Rome at that time, instigating conflict between the Jews and the Romans. If so, then it is worthless as a reference to Jesus.

Others, however, see the word Chestus as a variant spelling of Christ. It is not clear whether Suetonius actually thought this Chestus was personally in Rome or whether it was his followers causing the problems. At any rate, it tells us nothing new about Jesus or about the early Christians.

Suetonius wrote elsewhere about Christians who had come to Rome.

> Punishment by Nero was inflicted on the Christians, a class of men given to a new and mischievous superstition (*Lives of the Caesars*, 26.2).

He testified that Christians had come to Rome at an early date and their numbers were large enough to make them noticed. This is consistent with what we know from the Book of Acts.

LUCIAN (SECOND CENTURY)

The Greek satirist Lucian, who lived in the second century, alluded to Jesus. He wrote the following words.

> The man who was crucified in Palestine because he introduced this new cult into the world. . . Furthermore, their first lawgiver persuaded them that they were all brothers one of another after they have transgressed once for all by denying the Greek gods and by worshiping that crucified sophist himself and living under his laws (*On the Death of Peregrine*).

Lucian confirmed the New Testament record that Jesus Christ had died in Israel by means of crucifixion. We also find that Jesus was worshipped by His followers.

THE VALUE OF THESE WRITINGS

These are some of the early references, from non-Jewish sources, that testify to the existence of Jesus Christ, and His followers. As we can readily see, the references are limited, and are not of a firsthand nature. Therefore, they cannot be of much help in establishing any reliable information about Him. However, what we do have is consistent with the New Testament portrait of Jesus.

SUMMARY TO QUESTION 4
WHAT DO EARLY, NON-JEWISH, WRITINGS TELL US ABOUT JESUS? (EXTRA-BIBLICAL GENTILE SOURCES)

The question of the existence of Jesus Christ is really not in doubt. Not only do we have the first-hand sources from the New Testament, which tell us about His life and ministry, there are also Jewish writings which give further confirmation.

Add to this, the existence of Jesus is confirmed by a number of non-Jewish or Gentile writings. These individuals did not endorse the ministry of Jesus. In fact, they tried, without success, to stop Christianity from growing. In all of these efforts, however, we never find them denying Jesus' existence.

From non-Jewish sources we find a number of things which corroborate the New Testament.

For one thing, they say that Christ's public ministry began during the reign of Tiberius Caesar. This confirms the account given in the New Testament.

These sources also tell us that Pontius Pilate was governor of Judea at the time of Christ's death. Again, we find that this is a confirmation of what the New Testament says.

Also in accord with the New Testament, we find that Jesus was put to death as a criminal. Indeed, all four gospels give the same testimony.

Furthermore, these secular sources testify that His death occurred in Judea. This fits with the geography of the New Testament.

We are also informed that Jesus' death stopped the "superstition" for a short time but it soon broke out again. All of these facts confirm what is written in the New Testament.

Thus, from the New Testament, the Jewish sources, and the non-Jewish sources, we can confidently say that the issue of Jesus' existence is not an issue at all.

In fact, every source, friendly and unfriendly, testified that He existed. We find no one denying that He lived, or that He performed mighty deeds, or that He said the things attributed to Him in the New Testament.

Therefore, we should conclude the existence of Jesus Christ as an historical character is really beyond all doubt.

What Do The Early Christian Sources, Apart From the New Testament, Tell Us About Jesus? (Extra-Biblical Christian Sources)

Today, we have an early Jewish source, the writings of Josephus, which testifies to the existence of Jesus, as well as to the existence of the early church. We also possess fragmentary references to Jesus among non-Jewish writers. However, none of these references are from people who lived at the same time as Jesus.

There is something else that we must take into consideration—the writings of early Christians. What do they add, if anything, to our knowledge of Jesus?

THERE IS EARLY TESTIMONY FROM THE APOSTOLIC FATHERS

Apart from the New Testament, we have some early testimony from believers about Jesus' words and deeds. The earliest sources we possess are known as the "Apostolic Fathers." The Apostolic Fathers were individuals who personally knew some of the disciples of Jesus. While they were not Jesus' disciples, they were disciples of the disciples. They include the writings of Clement, Ignatius, Papias, and Polycarp. These writings were composed from about A.D. 95 to A.D. 150.

We discover the following from their writings.

1. CLEMENT OF ROME

There is an early letter that is called I Clement. It was written around the year A.D. 95 by Clement of Rome. He is probably the same one who is mentioned in the New Testament. When Paul wrote to the Philippians we find the following reference.

> Yes, I say also to you, true companion, help them. They have struggled together in the gospel ministry along with me and Clement and my other coworkers, whose names are in the book of life (Philippians 4:3 NET).

In his letter, Clement urged his readers to remember the sayings of Jesus. He calls them "the words of the Lord Jesus." He also cites certain statements of Jesus that are found in Matthew and Luke.

2. IGNATIUS OF ANTIOCH

Ignatius, the bishop of Antioch in Syria, is a very important early witness to Jesus. He was martyred for his faith in Christ under the reign of the Roman Emperor Trajan. This occurred before the year A.D. 117.

Ignatius wrote seven letters that have survived. In them, we find a number of key truths emphasized.

For one thing, Ignatius emphasizes that the Christian faith is based upon historical facts. He mentions how Jesus was crucified under the reign of Pontius Pilate and that He rose from the dead. Ignatius also wrote that those who believed in Jesus would also be raised one day.

In his writings, we find both the humanity and deity of Christ stressed. At that time, there was a heresy called "Docetism" that claimed that Jesus was not really human but only *seemed* to be human. Ignatius combated this false belief with his emphasis on the true humanity of Jesus as well as His deity.

There is something else. Ignatius is an example of another constant theme we find among the early believers in Jesus—he was willing to be martyred for his faith. Time and time again we find the early Christians persecuted, tortured and martyred for their beliefs in Jesus. Some explanation has to be given as to why all of them willingly went to their deaths proclaiming His message. One obvious conclusion is that they certainly believed the message they were proclaiming.

Therefore, we have an early testimony by a leader in the church which confirms some of the main teachings of the New Testament. Like others in the early church, Ignatius' citations or allusions came mainly from Matthew's gospel. Indeed, it was the favorite one in the early church.

3. PAPIAS

Papias had heard John the Apostle preach about Jesus. He was also a friend of Polycarp, the bishop of Smyrna. He knew the written accounts of the life of Jesus, as well as the oral tradition that was being taught about the Lord.

We are also told that he learned from the daughters of Philip the Apostle about a man being brought back to life in Philip's time. Papias was, therefore, in a position to relate both the written words, as well as the oral tradition, that was circulating about Jesus at his time.

4. POLYCARP

Polycarp was a disciple of the Apostle John. He was familiar with the letters of Paul as well as the words of Jesus. He is an important witness since he was a personal disciple of John. Therefore, he was taught directly by one who was personally taught by Jesus. At an old age, he was martyred for his faith in Jesus.

This briefly sums up what we know from the testimony of the early Christian sources or apostolic fathers. From them, we find further confirmatory evidence of the life and ministry of Christ.

SUMMARY TO QUESTION 5
WHAT DO THE EARLY CHRISTIAN SOURCES, APART FROM THE NEW TESTAMENT, TELL US ABOUT JESUS? (EXTRA-BIBLICAL CHRISTIAN SOURCES)

The early Christian sources, outside of the New Testament, corroborate the story of Jesus found in Scripture. There are four important individuals who are worth mentioning.

First, we have the testimony the testimony of Clement of Rome—a man mentioned in the New Testament. He testified about the life and deeds of Jesus.

Two other men, Polycarp and Papias had personal contact with John the Apostle. Thus, they were only one generation removed from Jesus Himself. Indeed, they were in a position to relate the accounts of an eyewitness to the events in the life of Christ.

Add to this the testimony of Ignatius of Antioch. He emphasized some of the key truths of the New Testament—such as the full humanity as well as the deity of Jesus Christ.

These writers not only testify to the existence of Jesus they also corroborate parts of the New Testament. In sum, these early writings, by men who were personally acquainted with Jesus' disciples, add further testimony to the fact of Jesus' existence.

What Do The Combined Ancient Sources, Jewish, Non-Jewish, And Christian, Say About Jesus? (Biblical And Extra-Biblical Evidence)

There is ancient testimony about Jesus Christ from a number of sources. However, the only firsthand evidence which we have comes from the New Testament. Its portrayal of Jesus is clear.

According to the New Testament, Jesus, the man from Nazareth, is actually God the Son, Second Person of the Holy Trinity, who became a human being at a certain point in history. He was born a Jew, performed certain miraculous deeds, including healings and exorcism of demons, as He preached the arrival of God's kingdom. He was rejected by the Jewish leadership and died the shameful death of crucifixion under the Roman governor Pontius Pilate. Jesus was then buried.

However, this was not the end. Indeed, Jesus, the carpenter from Nazareth rose from the dead three days after His death! He appeared numerous times to His disciples after His resurrection from the dead. Soon thereafter, He ascended into heaven.

Then His followers began to spread His message. They started in Jerusalem and continued throughout the Roman Empire. The belief in Jesus spread rapidly. About thirty years after the death of Jesus, a large number of Christians were in Rome. These first believers worshipped Jesus as the one true God who had become a human being.

These are some of the core truths of the New Testament.

What is important to realize is that all of these essential truths are confirmed by early sources outside of the New Testament. We can make the following observations.

1. ALL EARLY SOURCES CONFIRM THE ESSENTIALS OF THE NEW TESTAMENT

Apart from the New Testament, we have other ancient sources that mention Jesus and His ministry. They include Jewish writings, non-Jewish writings, and the writings of the early Christians. If we combine the testimony of these various early sources, we find a portrait of Jesus that is consistent with what is revealed in the New Testament. This is of extreme importance. It tells us that every ancient source agreed on a number of things about Jesus, His ministry, the experience of the early Christians, and the spread of Christianity.

2. THE SOURCES NEVER DENY JESUS' EXISTENCE OR HIS MIRACLES

In addition, it is also important to note what these writings do not say. Every source admits that Jesus existed and every source that spoke of His ministry testified to some sort of mighty deeds. Consequently, we have no denial of His existence, neither do we have any denials that He performed spectacular works. In sum, the enemies of the faith never denied Jesus' existence or His miracles.

3. THERE IS NO BASIS TO BELIEVE THE STORY HAD BEEN CHANGED

Because of the consistent testimony from all sources, both friendly and unfriendly, there is no historical basis to argue that the real story of Jesus was somehow suppressed or changed.

It is often alleged that the later Christians rewrote the story of Jesus and made Him into something that He never was. However, since all the ancient sources corroborate the New Testament's version of Jesus' claims, this argument cannot be sustained.

4. THE NEW TESTAMENT ACCOUNT OF JESUS MUST BE TAKEN SERIOUSLY

Therefore, from the evidence we possess, we have every reason to accept the story of Jesus, as it has been revealed in the New Testament, as representing what actually occurred. Jesus was an historical figure who existed and did certain things. All sources agree on this fact. They all agree that Christians believed Jesus to be a miracle worker, the promised Messiah, and One who rose from the dead.

Obviously there has to be some basis as to why they held this belief. This is the issue that must be faced. Whether of not one believes in Jesus as God the Son, we know that the early Christians believed it.

The question then arises, "Why did they believe this?" What caused them to hold onto these beliefs, to evangelize the entire Roman Empire with the message of the risen Jesus, and, in so many cases, to die a horrible death because of their belief? Something obviously caused them to do all of this. What was it?

5. SOME EXPLANATION MUST BE GIVEN FOR THE RAPID SPREAD OF CHRISTIANITY

If the New Testament explanation is not the true one, then some type of explanation must be given to explain why Christianity spread so rapidly in the ancient world. Its immediate spread to all parts of the Roman Empire is a fact of history that all agree upon. People from all walks of life, rich and poor, young and old, intellectuals and non-intellectuals, embraced the message of Jesus. They gave up everything to follow Him.

The question that has to be answered is, "Why?" What made it spread like it did? Why did so many Jewish people immediately embrace a leader who was brutally executed by Rome? Something monumental caused this to occur. The New Testament is clear about the reason why. Indeed, the crucified Messiah rose from the dead!

SUMMARY TO QUESTION 6
WHAT DO THE COMBINED ANCIENT SOURCES, JEWISH, NON-JEWISH, AND CHRISTIAN, SAY ABOUT JESUS? (BIBLICAL AND EXTRA-BIBLICAL EVIDENCE)

It is important to realize that every ancient source which touches upon the life and ministry of Jesus corroborates the New Testament account of Him, His ministry, and the experiences of the early Christians.

In fact, not only do these sources verify the essentials of the New Testament, none of them deny Jesus' existence or His miraculous deeds.

Furthermore, there is no basis whatsoever, of assuming that the real story of Jesus was somehow hidden or suppressed. While many people would like to believe that we do not have to face the New Testament claims about Jesus, the facts say otherwise.

Finally, some explanation needs to be given to explain why the belief in Jesus spread so rapidly. The secular world cannot give us that explanation but the Scripture certainly can! The message of Jesus was, and is, the message of the living God.

QUESTION 7

What Do The Dead Sea Scrolls
Tell Us About Jesus' Existence?

The most amazing archaeological find of the twentieth century, as far as the Bible is concerned, was the discovery of the Dead Sea Scrolls. What, if anything, do they tell us about Jesus? What do we need to know about them?

WHAT ARE THE DEAD SEA SCROLLS?

The Dead Sea Scrolls is the name given to a number of manuscripts that were hidden in caves in Israel in a place called Qumran. The caves were located about five hundred yards from the southeastern corner of the Dead Sea. The written texts were composed from 150 B.C. to A.D. 68 when the Romans destroyed the settlement. The opinion of most scholars is that the texts were written and copied by a strict Jewish community known as the Essenes.

THERE HAVE BEEN BIZARRE THEORIES AND SENSATIONAL CLAIMS

Because of the nature of the discovery, it was inevitable that people would come up with some bizarre theories about the meaning of the scrolls, and their importance to the origins of the Christian faith. When the scrolls were first discovered, and their contents made known, a number of sensational claims were made concerning them. Some claimed to find hidden references to Jesus among the scrolls while others claimed the scrolls showed Christianity derived from the teachings of the Essene community.

While some of these theories have been given wide reportage in the popular press, sane biblical scholarship has ignored them. Rather than repeating the various theories, and the people responsible for them, we will merely note that a number of outlandish theories about the scrolls have surfaced over the years.

THE TEACHER OF RIGHTEOUSNESS WAS SUPPOSEDLY RAISED FROM THE DEAD

There were claims in the early 1950's, from one of first scholars who studied the scrolls, that a person mentioned in the scrolls, known as the Teacher of Righteousness, was actually a forerunner, in a sense to Jesus. Supposedly, this Teacher of Righteousness was tortured to death but then supernaturally re-appeared after he died. These claims caused an immediate stir. Did the Dead Sea Scrolls actually speak of a dying and rising Teacher? Did the writers of the New Testament merely borrow the idea of a risen Teacher from the Dead Sea Scrolls?

However, this identification was soon shown to be incorrect. The verb translated "re-appear" can better be translated "appear." Thus, nothing supernatural is involved. In addition, most scholars understand the subject of the verb to be the Wicked Priest, not the Teacher of Righteousness. Therefore, we do not find any resurrection predicted for the "Teacher of Righteousness."

THE TEACHER OF RIGHTEOUSNESS WAS SUPPOSEDLY CRUCIFIED

Another sensational theory soon arose from another one of those individuals who had been given the responsibility of publishing the text. This man said the Teacher of Righteousness had been crucified. This scholar went on to claim that the Gospel story of Jesus was mere fiction based upon the example of the Teacher of Righteousness.

This theory too was rejected by other scholars who worked on the scrolls. They pointed out that there is nothing taught in the scrolls which say the Teacher of Righteousness was crucified. Thus, what we find was not information, but rather disinformation from those who had no interest in truth but rather wanted to destroy the foundations of Christianity. As always happens, these attempts miserably fail.

THE BIZARRE CLAIMS CONTINUED

These types of claims did not cease in the 1950's and 1960's. The scrolls were entrusted to a select group of scholars who had exclusive control over their publication. As the decades went by, very few of the scrolls were actually published.

The scandal of the lack of publication of the Dead Sea Scrolls was becoming more and more evident. Why wasn't the public, or even other scholars, allowed to look at certain texts? In that climate, there were a number of allegations of a cover-up. Supposedly, the Roman Catholic Church, which had a number of scholars in charge of certain scrolls, was keeping their contents hidden from the public.

Eventually, a set of photos of the scrolls was published. This allowed scholars to see what had been hidden from view for all of these years. There were no sensational finds, no cover-ups, and no mention of Jesus. In other words, there was no historical bombshell.

DO THE SCROLLS SPEAK OF A PIERCED MESSIAH?

However, one scholar did create something of a stir when he claimed that one particular fragment, that was newly made public, actually spoke of the Messiah being "pierced." This fragment, was part of a document called the "War Scroll," which spoke of the coming Messiah. Again, the claim was made that Christianity derived its teachings from the Dead Sea Scrolls, or that the scrolls were actually written by Jews who had become involved with Jesus and His ministry. The origins of Christianity were once more challenged.

Scholarship, yet again, showed that these claims were unfounded. The War Scroll, in its context, speaks of the Messiah as someone who is triumphant, not someone who suffers. Thus, there is no justification for the translation that the Messiah was "pierced."

Therefore, when all the evidence is in, we have no real connection, or anticipation, between Jesus and this Teacher mentioned in the scrolls. Neither do we have to revise our view of Christian origins because of information found in the scrolls.

MORE ALLEGATIONS THAT CHRISTIANITY DERIVED ITS TEACHINGS FROM THE SCROLLS

Other allegations were made that the teachings of the New Testament regarding Jesus were not unique at all. Supposedly, Jesus spent His youth among the Essenes and learned His doctrine from them. In addition, John the Baptist was said to have derived his beliefs from this community. Parallels were found between New Testament teachings and the teachings of the Essenes. Conclusions were drawn that the New Testament teaching owed its ideas to those at Qumran—not the living God.

Again, we find these allegations to be completely false. There is no indication, whatsoever, that Jesus, or John the Baptist, had any contact with the Essenes. Even if they had, there is certainly no reason to believe they were influenced by these teachings. A close examination of the teachings of the Essenes, and the New Testament, show them to be in conflict in many central areas.

THE CLAIM THAT FRAGMENTS OF THE NEW TESTAMENT WERE FOUND AMONG THE SCROLLS

In 1972, a sensational claim was made, by a reputable scholar, which said portions of the New Testament were found among the Dead Sea Scrolls. Jose O'Callaghan, a noted expert in the study of piecing together ancient texts, believed he discovered a portion of the Gospel of Mark from a small fragment found in Cave Seven. This particular cave is unique in the sense that all the fragments found were written in Greek—not Hebrew and Aramaic like the remainder of the scrolls.

While his reconstruction has not convinced most scholars, there are still a number of world-class experts who believe that his theory is possible. The best we can say is that it has not been proven that any part of the New Testament has been discovered among the scrolls. However, O'Callaghan's reconstruction is not impossible.

THERE IS NOTHING DIRECTLY SAID ABOUT JESUS IN THE DEAD SEA SCROLLS

We conclude that the Dead Sea Scrolls do not directly mention Jesus Christ. In fact, it seems that most, if not all, of the scrolls were written before Jesus' public ministry. While there have been claims that parts of the New Testament were found in one of the caves, Cave Seven, this has never been widely accepted by scholars.

SUMMARY TO QUESTION 7
WHAT DO THE DEAD SEA SCROLLS TELL US ABOUT JESUS' EXISTENCE?

The Dead Sea Scrolls is the popular description of a group of manuscripts which were found in the late 1940's some five hundred yards from the southeastern corner of the Dead Sea. Contained within the Dead Sea Scrolls are fragments from every Old Testament book except Esther. These manuscripts were one thousand years older than any previous manuscript which scholars used to reconstruct the Old Testament text. It was the archaeological find of the century.

Important as the Dead Sea Scrolls are, they tell us absolutely nothing about Jesus or His disciples. Indeed, they provide no firsthand information about Him, or His ministry. No New Testament characters are mentioned in the scrolls. Most likely they were all written before the life and ministry of Jesus. Thus, we should not expect to find anything about Him in the scrolls.

The discovery of the scrolls caused a number of sensational claims to be made about them and the origin of Christianity. However, none of these outlandish claims turned out to be true. Indeed, nothing that has been found among the Dead Sea Scrolls would cause us to change what the New Testament says about Jesus. Neither do the scrolls provide any basis for the eccentric claims that certain people have made.

What they do provide is information about one particular group that lived during the time of Jesus. They were known as the Essenes.

In sum, from the Dead Scrolls, we have a better understanding of the world in which Jesus came. However, they have no direct bearing on what Jesus said or did.

Why Don't We Have More Early Sources Referring To Jesus?

While the secular sources do tell us that Jesus Christ existed, there are some common objections that arise when this subject is brought up. They include the following.

First, it is asked why Jesus wasn't more noticed by historians of the time. If He was such a great figure, then why don't we have more written about Him? If Jesus did what the New Testament says that He did, then why didn't other writers living at the time mention it?

In addition, why do the references, that we do possess, contain so little detail? If He did the sort of the things which the New Testament said He did, then shouldn't we expect more specific things to have been written?

How do we respond to questions like these? There are several observations that should be made.

1. WE HAVE LIMITED KNOWLEDGE OF THAT PERIOD

First, we must realize that our knowledge of the first century A.D. is limited. The majority of books that were written in the ancient world have not survived.

For example, the Roman Emperor Claudius wrote thirty-seven books— but not one of them survives. We only know the existence of his works, as well as other lost books, through references and quotations from them found in other works. Therefore, our knowledge of any historical figure, or event in the ancient world, is limited by the lack of existing sources.

Furthermore, the very few writings that have survived are only fragmentary. Therefore, we should not expect to find much information about any figure living at that time. The information is just not there. Consequently, the shortage of ancient testimony about Jesus should not surprise us.

2. RELIGIOUS FIGURES WERE NOT THE MAIN SUBJECT OF ANCIENT WRITERS

We should also note that most of the figures who received any notice in ancient writings were political and military figures—not religious leaders. They were not really noticed by the writers of their day. This being the case, we certainly should not expect the writers to have written anything about Jesus and the claims which were made for Him.

For example, it is often wondered why John the Baptist is mentioned by first-century Jewish historian Josephus more than he mentions Jesus. The answer lies in the purpose of Josephus. Josephus is mainly interested in writing about the political history of the Jews. John would have figured more importantly because he spoke out against King Herod. In fact, the gospels tell us this is the reason Herod put John into prison.

On the other hand, Jesus did not engage in political speech. We find that He would not be drawn into a discussion about paying taxes to Caesar.

In addition, He agreed to pay the poll tax. Indeed, the movement of Jesus was not a political movement. Hence, we do not have more than a passing mention to Him.

3. THE WRITERS WOULD NOT HAVE IMMEDIATELY FORESEEN HIS IMPACT

There is more. We should not expect these ancient writers to have foreseen the influence that Jesus would have had on the world. There is no way in which they could have known the impact that He would have made.

Therefore, we should not expect them to carefully document the life and ministry of Jesus—seeing they had no idea of how Christianity would develop. Many new religions sprung up in the Roman Empire and to them Christianity was just another one of the many.

4. JESUS LIVED IN A REMOTE AREA OF THE ROMAN EMPIRE

There is another thing to keep in mind. Judea was in a remote part of the eastern Empire. This particular geographical region held little importance for Rome. The fact that some religious figure was executed would not have been that exceptional.

Indeed, first century writer Flavius Josephus tells us that about two thousand Jewish insurgents were put to death after disturbances following the death of Herod the Great in approximately 3–2 B.C. Therefore, the death of a single religious figure, in this remote area of the Empire, would not have been a cause for much notice in Rome—no matter what had been claimed about Him.

What we would expect is that the growth of the Christian movement outside of Judea would have attracted the attention of ancient writers. This is exactly what we find. As Christianity grew in number, it began to be noticed by those writing of the events of the time.

5. MANY DID NOT BELIEVE IN HIM DURING HIS LIFETIME

There is something else. The gospels tell us that many people who heard Jesus, including members of His own family, did not believe in Him. John records that during His public ministry, the brothers of Jesus did not believe in Him.

For even His brothers did not believe in Him (John 7:5 NKJV).

Since they did not believe in Jesus during His public ministry, we should not expect others to take notice.

THE KEY ISSUE: HOW RELIABLE ARE THE SOURCES?

The real issue concerns the reliability of the sources. The key question is, "How accurate is the information that the historian gives us?" The fact that Jesus is not mentioned in any contemporary non-Christian source does not prove He did not exist.

Given what we know about ancient writers, and the fact that very few writings from the ancient world have survived, it is not surprising we find such little information about Jesus from secular sources.

WE HAVE SUFFICIENT TESTIMONY ABOUT JESUS

We must emphasize that there are non-Christian sources that mention Jesus' life and ministry. They are sufficient to testify that Jesus Himself did exist. Not only do we have the firsthand eyewitnesses' testimony of the New Testament, there are also these secular sources that confirm many of the events recorded in the New Testament.

Consequently, we conclude that Jesus was an historical figure whose existence is beyond all doubt. Both the secular sources, and the New Testament, give evidence of His existence.

Therefore, the objection—that the non-Christian evidence about Jesus is too little and too late—does not hold any weight. Jesus of Nazareth did exist and there are many things that we can know about His life and ministry.

SUMMARY TO QUESTION 8
WHY DON'T WE HAVE MORE EARLY SOURCES REFERRING TO JESUS?

One issue which often comes up with respect to Jesus Christ and His ministry concerns the lack of written sources from people of His own era. Indeed, we do not find Jesus mentioned by contemporary historians. At least, nothing has survived that was written about Jesus by ancient historians living at His time.

Given the extraordinary things that the New Testament says that He did, shouldn't we expect to see more references? Furthermore, why don't the few references we do have about Him give us more details? Why is there so little written about Him? Why don't we find more?

This is really not surprising. In fact, the non-Christian evidence is what we would expect to find from the sources that we have. It is wrong to expect them to say more about Jesus. A number of points need to be made.

For one thing, there are few sources that still exist from His time. Consequently, there is very little from that time period that we can examine. The great majority of the written records have been lost.

In addition, at that time in history, those people who were written about were more political and military figures rather than religious figures. This is another reason for the lack of information—the religious leaders were not given much exposure.

Furthermore, they would not have known the impact that His life was going to make. Indeed, who at that time could have foreseen the effect that Jesus would make upon the world? This being the case, it is understandable why His life and ministry would have been overlooked.

There is also the geographical problem. Jesus would have not attracted that much attention living and ministering in far off Israel. Consequently, the location of His life and ministry tended to not make Him a topic of discussion among current writers.

Add to this the fact that these secular people would not have believed in Him. Most writers would have probably considered Jesus as another religious leader about whom great claims were made. This is a further reason why we find nothing written from these historians.

The important point is that we *do* have accurate testimony about the life and ministry of Jesus from firsthand sources. This is found in the New Testament. It gives us a correct portrait of who Jesus is, as well as what He accomplished during His time on the earth.

The fact that secular writers, for the most part, tended to ignore Him is not really relevant. Indeed, what we do have is the testimony of the eyewitnesses. They are the ones who tell us what Jesus said and did. Furthermore, their testimony is trustworthy.

What Year Was Jesus Born?

While we know Jesus actually existed, the exact year in which He was born is a subject of dispute. There have been various theories as to the precise year of His birth.

There are a number of important points that need to be made about this issue.

THE TIME BEFORE AND AFTER JESUS CHRIST

After the Roman Empire became Christianized, an attempt was made to date events before, and after, the birth of Christ. Our calendars today recognize the fact of Jesus' coming to the world. The letters B.C. stands for "before Christ." The letters A.D. is the Latin Anno Domini, which stands for "In the year of our Lord."

HEROD THE GREAT WAS STILL ALIVE WHEN JESUS WAS BORN

We know that Jesus Christ was born some time before the death of King Herod. It was Herod who sent the Magi to find the place where the Christ had been born (Matthew 2). Herod later sent the soldiers to slaughter the innocents of Bethlehem (Matthew 2). Therefore, whenever Jesus was born it was sometime before Herod's death.

HOW COULD CHRIST HAVE BEEN BORN B.C.?

In modern times, the death of Herod has been commonly believed to have occurred in the year 4 B.C. Recently, however, there has been evidence brought forward to revise the date to 2-3 B.C.

Andrew Steinmann, who has written a monumental work on biblical chronology, concluded the following about the birth of Jesus after examining all the relevant evidence.

> Since we have now established that Herod died early in 1 BC after January 10 but before Passover (April 8), we can now confirm that Jesus was born no earlier than midyear 3 BC and no later than the end of 2 BC. Given the events surrounding Jesus' birth we can surmise that at least a few months passed between Jesus' birth and Herod's death. The arrival of the magi in Jerusalem was after Jesus' birth, but before Herod's death (Matt 2:1). Herod waited some time for the Magi to return before ordering execution of the boys of Bethlehem (Matt 2:16). Since he ordered the execution of boys up to two years old, matching the time when the magi indicated they had first seen the star (Matt 2:7,16) the magi first observed the star no earlier than about 4 BC. Joseph and Mary's flight to Egypt with the infant Jesus shortly after the visit of the Magi (Matt 2:13-15) should probably be dated after mid-2 BC and no later than early 1 BC. (Andrew Steinmann, *From Abraham To Paul*, Concordia Press, p. 238).

If this is the case, then Christ had to have been born sometime before 2 B.C? How can this be? How could Christ have been born before Himself?

HISTORY'S GREATEST MATHEMATICAL ERROR

The source of this problem goes back to a sixth century Roman monk/ mathematician named Dionysius Exiguus (Dionysius the little). In attempting to calculate the year of the birth of Christ, this monk made a simple error that had profound implications. Dionysius dated the birth of Christ as 753 years from the founding of Rome.

The problem with this calculation is that Herod seems to have died only 751 years after Rome's founding. Since Herod was still alive after Christ was born, we seem to have an error of about two years. Though Dionysius gave the correct date for the founding of Rome, he was incorrect in his calculations for the birth of Christ. The chronology of Dionysius was incorporated into our calendars with the miscalculation about the birth of Christ undiscovered.

THE SAME ERROR IS FOUND TODAY

To this day, our calendars reflect this error. Thus, the birth of Christ probably occurred sometime in the years 3/2 B.C., a couple of years before Himself!

Consequently, if we are adding up the years from Christ's birth, until the present year, we need to add about two years to our current calendar year to get the approximate date of when He was born. Thus, the year 2000 would have actually been more like 2002 years from the birth of Christ.

We must emphasize that this miscalculation is not a mistake in the Bible. Indeed, the Bible does not give us the exact year when our Lord was born. The miscalculation came hundreds of years later. The important point in all of this is that Jesus Christ, God the Son, was indeed born into our world.

SUMMARY TO QUESTION 9
WHAT YEAR WAS JESUS BORN?

As to the exact year in which Jesus was born, we do not know. It was obviously before the death of King Herod seeing that it was Herod who sent the Magi to Bethlehem to find where the Christ Child was located. Later, Herod ordered the slaughter of the innocent babes of Bethlehem.

The most likely date of Jesus' birth is now assumed to be somewhere from 3-2 B.C. Because of the error of Dionysius Exiguus, the sixth century monk/mathematician, our calendars are off by about two years. This man was commissioned to determine what year Christ was born and it seems that he made an error in his calculations of approximately two years.

Thus, to calculate the date when Christ was born from our present calendars, we should probably add about two years to our current year to have the approximate year He was born.

This error, we should stress, is not a mistake of the Bible. It is, rather, a miscalculation made in the sixth century A.D. in an attempt to date the birth of Christ. The Bible itself does not give the exact year for the birth of Christ. What we do know is that Jesus Christ, the Savior of the world, did come as promised.

Was Jesus Born
On December 25th?

Not only has the exact year of Jesus Christ's birth been a matter of debate, the exact date of the birth of Jesus is also something that is far from settled. In the Western world, December 25th is the date set aside to celebrate the birth of Jesus. The early church in the West seems to have celebrated the birth of Christ on December 25th while the church in the East observed January 6th.

While we cannot be certain of the exact date there are a number of things that we do know. They include the following.

WAS THE DATE OF THE BIRTH OF CHRIST SUBSTITUTED FOR A PAGAN FESTIVAL?

During that time in history, the Romans celebrated the Saturnalia festival on December 25th. This marked the date of the winter solstice—the time when the sun would turn northward again. The feast was called Sol Invictus, the "Unconquerable Sun." It is alleged that the Christians at that time wanted to replace the pagan festivals with Christian festivals. Since the phrase "Son of Righteousness" was a common designation for Jesus, it seemed natural to celebrate this date as the birth of the Son of Righteousness rather than celebrating the Unconquerable Sun in the sky.

Therefore, it is argued, that the selection of December 25th, as the date of the birth of Jesus Christ, was a matter of substitution of the Christian festival for a pagan festival.

THE CHRISTIANS HELD THIS DATE EARLIER

Yet this does not seem to be the case. In fact, there is compelling evidence that Christians celebrated December 25th as the date of Jesus' birth *before* the pagans adopted this date. This would mean that the Romans actually used December 25th to counteract the Christian celebration of the birth of Christ.

Joseph Kelly writes the following.

> In 274 Aurelian [the Roman emperor at that time] instituted the cult of Sol Invictus, the Unconquered Sun....Aurelian made December 25, the winter solstice, the birthday of Sol Invictus and thus a major feast day throughout the Roman Empire....
>
> In 336 the local church at Rome proclaimed December 25 as the dies natalis Christi, 'the natal day of Christ,' that is, his birthday. The document which says this does not justify or explain it. It merely says that this is the day, that is, the date had been accepted by the Roman church some time before and since everyone knew about it, discussion of the date was not necessary.
>
> But how long before 336 was the date for Christmas accepted? Historians have wondered whether the Christians in the late third century had waged a propaganda war against Aurelian, promoting their Sun of Righteousness [This refers Jesus in the context of Malachi 4:2], the Sol Iustitiae against his Unconquered Sun, the Sol Invictus....
>
> We should also recall that Sextus Julius Africanus [a Christian author who wrote during the first half of the third century]

had already proposed December 25 as the date of Christ's birth. Aurelian's opponents may have plausibly reasoned that if the date already existed [in Christian circles], why not use it against the imperial cult of the Sun?...

The second piece of evidence for a third-century propaganda struggle is a work of art, a mosaic on the ceiling of a tomb of the family Julii and now preserved in the necropolis (Greek for 'city of the dead') under St. Peter's basilica in Rome. It portrays Christ driving a chariot through the heavens, just as the pagan sun god Helios did, and Jesus, like the god, has rays of light emanating from his head....

They date the mosaic to the late third century, that is, at the time when the emperor Aurelian was promoting the cult of the Unconquered Sun. Significantly, this is the only ancient portrayal of Christ as the sun. Historians find it impossible to believe that this portrayal was just coincidentally produced in the city of Rome at the very time when the pagans were promoting the cult of their sun (Joseph Kelly, *The Origins Of Christmas* [Collegeville, Minnesota: Liturgical Press, 2004], pp. 65-68).

In support of this, the Encyclopaedia Britannica notes.

December 25 was first identified as the date of Jesus' birth by Sextus Julius Africanus in 221...by a priori reasoning that identified the spring equinox...as the day of Jesus' conception...March 25... December 25, nine months later, then became the date of Jesus' birth ("Christmas," *Encyclopaedia Britannica*, 2008).

Therefore, the common belief, that the church took December 25th as the birth of Christ from an already established pagan holiday, seems itself to be a myth.

IT WAS COMMONLY BELIEVED THAT CHRIST WAS BORN IN MID-WINTER

What we do know is that the exact date of Jesus' birth is not stated in the New Testament. It is most commonly believed that Jesus was born sometime during either the fall, or winter, with mid-winter being a popular view. Thus, December 25th could have been the exact date when Jesus was born since December is winter in the northern hemisphere.

In fact, Andrew Steinmann, whom we cited as an authority on biblical chronology in the previous question, listed Jesus' birth as either "Late 3 or early 2 [BC]" (Steinmann p. 254). December 25th fits that time frame.

However, there is simply not enough evidence to be certain. Consequently, exact precision as to when Jesus was born seems to be impossible. Yet, December 25th seems to be a definite possibility.

OBJECTION: WHAT ABOUT THE FLOCKS BEING OUTSIDE IN WINTER?

One objection to the date of December 25th is that the shepherds are tending their flocks by night when the announcement comes of the birth of Christ. It is argued that it would be too cold for them to have their flocks outside in the winter. Therefore, it must have been some other time of year. However, this often-used argument does not hold much weight. There is evidence, both ancient and modern, that flocks stayed outside year round.

THERE IS ANCIENT EVIDENCE THAT FLOCKS WERE OUTSIDE ALL YEAR ROUND IN BETHLEHEM

There is a passage in the Jewish Mishnah that stated that some sheep were kept outside of the fields of Bethlehem all year round. These sheep were to be used for sacrifice in the temple in Jerusalem. Therefore, it is possible that the birth of Jesus could have come on any day of the year —including December 25th.

THERE IS MODERN EVIDENCE OF FLOCKS OUTSIDE IN WINTER

Shepherds in the Bethlehem area, to this very day, keep their flocks out at night during all times of the year. Anyone visiting Bethlehem around Christmas time can still see the sheep outside with the shepherds.

CONCLUSION: THE BIRTH OF CHRIST COULD HAVE BEEN IN WINTER

It would, therefore, not be impossible for the birth of Jesus to have occurred during the winter season. Based upon the present evidence, a December to mid-January date somewhere around the year 3/2 B.C. seems to be the preferred time for the birth of Jesus.

SUMMARY TO QUESTION 10
WAS JESUS BORN ON DECEMBER 25TH?

As there is a question as to the exact year Jesus was born, the exact day of His birth is also uncertain. December 25th was chosen as the date in the West, while January 6th is the day it is celebrated by the Eastern Church.

It is commonly argued that the date December 25th came from substituting the pagan Roman festival around the winter solstice with the celebration of the birth of Christ. The Christians, it is alleged, substituted the birth of the "Son of Righteousness" for the "Unconquerable sun." However, the evidence seems to point in the opposite direction. The Christians actually celebrated December 25th as the date of Jesus birth before the Romans adopted that date.

Therefore, it is not the Christians that substituted the date of a pagan Roman holiday for the birth of Christ but rather the Romans adopted December 25th to counteract the Christian celebration of Jesus' birth.

While it is certainly possible that Jesus was born on that date, there is not enough evidence to be precise. We do know however, that He was born sometime in the past, with mid-winter somewhere around 3/2 B.C. being a possible date suggested by modern scholars.

As to the objection that mid-winter would be inappropriate because the flocks were kept outside at night, we find that even today the sheep are kept outside year-round in the Bethlehem area. Thus, mid-winter remains a possible time for His birth.

While we may never know the exact date of His birth, we do know for certain that Christ was indeed born in the city of Bethlehem as the prophet had said.

What Do We Know Of Jesus' Earlier Years

The New Testament gives us the only firsthand account of the life of Jesus Christ. We are told of the events surrounding His birth, and of His ministry to the world. But apart from one incident at age twelve, there is nothing told about His childhood, or anything that happened to Him until about age thirty. Several observations can be made about this silence on the part of Scripture.

1. THERE WAS THE DESIRE TO KNOW MORE

While the church viewed the gospels as the authoritative source for the life and ministry of Jesus, others felt the need to fill in the blanks of the things the Gospels do not speak of. This includes the childhood of Jesus, His physical appearance, and other sayings not recorded in the New Testament.

2. FANCIFUL STORIES AROSE ABOUT JESUS' EARLY YEARS

Throughout history, fanciful accounts of Jesus' youth have been written but all of these have proven unreliable. The only firsthand source we have about the life of Jesus is the New Testament, and it remains silent about Jesus' youth. Apocryphal sources attempt to fill in the gaps but they are not trustworthy.

AN EXAMPLE OF A FANCIFUL STORY ABOUT JESUS: THE ARABIC GOSPEL OF THE INFANCY

In the *Arabic Gospel of the Infancy* there is the romantic story of these silent years. We are told that when Joseph and Mary were on their way to Egypt with the baby Jesus, robbers met them. The robbers found nothing to steal from this couple because they did not have any money. The robbers had compassion on the young couple with their child and gave them provisions and sent them on their way to Egypt.

One of these helpful robbers appeared in the life of Christ many years later. He was the repentant criminal on the cross next to Jesus! Though this charming story has no basis whatsoever in fact, it illustrates the desire to fill in some of the missing elements in the story of Jesus.

3. THERE WERE NO MIRACLES BEFORE HIS PUBLIC MINISTRY BEGAN

We do know that Jesus did not perform any miraculous deeds before He began His public ministry. The Gospel of John testifies that the miracle of turning the water into wine was Jesus' first miracle. The Bible says the following.

> This was Jesus' first miracle, and he did it in the village of Cana in Galilee. There Jesus showed his glory, and his disciples put their faith in him (John 2:11 CEV).

Therefore, any account of a miracle by Jesus before this time would be inaccurate. His first miracle occurred in Cana of Galilee.

WHY DO WE HAVE SILENCE ABOUT JESUS' EARLIER YEARS?

This brings up the question of the silence of the Gospels on the early years of Jesus. Why the silence? Why doesn't the Scripture give us more details on the childhood and youth of Jesus? Although the Bible does not give us any specific information on Jesus' early years, we can surmise why it has remained virtually silent on the matter.

1. THE FOUR GOSPELS EMPHASIZED THE PUBLIC MINISTRY OF JESUS

The four Gospels basically record the life and ministry of Jesus to the world. They were not written as biographies, in the modern sense of the term, but as documents meaning to convey God's truth that Jesus was the Savior sent from heaven. They emphasize those events that prove that He was the Promised Messiah who came to earth. Elements of His life which do not deal with His public ministry are not recorded for us.

2. JESUS DID NOT BEGIN HIS PUBLIC MINISTRY UNTIL THE AGE OF THIRTY

The Gospels record that Jesus did not begin His public ministry until He was about thirty years of age. Luke records the following.

> So Jesus, when he began his ministry, was about thirty years
> old. He was the son (as was supposed) of Joseph, the son of
> Heli (Luke 3:23 NET)

Whatever happened to Jesus, before He began His public ministry, was time spent in preparation for what He was about to undertake. Consequently, the events of those years are not revealed in Scripture.

3. THESE SILENT YEARS WERE NOT UNIMPORTANT

But let us not think that these years of silence were unimportant years. Without a doubt Jesus was performing whatever duty that was set before Him with the same dedication He would later have in His ministry. His faithfulness is acknowledged at His baptism when God the Father's voice was heard.

> Then a voice from heaven said, "This is my own dear Son,
> and I am pleased with him" (Matthew 3:17 CEV).

There had been no miracles, no great teachings, nothing as yet on a grand scale. Yet we know that the Father was pleased with His Son. Whatever things Jesus did during those silent years, He did them very well. This means that His life was pleasing to His heavenly Father.

This is a great lesson for all of us. Indeed, not only does the Lord watch everything which we do, it is important that we be found faithful in everything.

Paul would later write to the Corinthians about this important truth. He put it this way.

> People should think of us as servants of Christ and managers who are entrusted with God's mysteries. Managers are required to be trustworthy (1 Corinthians 4:1,2 God's Word).

Like Jesus, we should desire to be found faithful—trustworthy, in all things.

In sum, though we may wish to know more about the early years of Jesus Christ, we can be satisfied with the knowledge that the youth of Jesus was spent being faithful to His calling.

We, as believers in Jesus, are also called to be faithful. John would later write.

> Whoever claims to live in him must walk as Jesus did (1 John 2:6 NIV).

Therefore, we should pattern our lives after His—a life of obedience to God the Father.

SUMMARY TO QUESTION 11
WHAT DO WE KNOW OF JESUS' EARLIER YEARS?

The Bible tells us very little about the life of Jesus before He began His public ministry. In fact, apart from the narratives around His birth, the only account we have of Him, before entering the ministry, was when He was at the temple at age twelve. Apart from that, the Scriptures are silent. Indeed, we know absolutely nothing about those years.

While the Scriptures are silent, others have attempted to fill in the gaps in these silent years. Yet their attempts really cannot be taken seriously. Indeed, the only reliable information we have about the life of Jesus Christ is found in the New Testament.

In fact, we know that He did not perform *any* miracles before turning the water into wine at Cana of Galilee. Scripture is explicit that this was His first miracle. Consequently, any account that has Him performing miracles as a child must be rejected.

This brings us to another important point. Although the years were silent as far as ministry was concerned they were still important years— they were preparing Jesus for the great things He was about to do. Therefore, while these may have been silent years, they certainly were not wasted years.

In addition, we know that whatever Jesus did during that time it was well-pleasing to God the Father. Indeed, when Jesus was baptized, the voice of God the Father stated that He was pleased with His beloved Son. Yet Jesus had not even begun His public ministry. To sum up, before there were any miracles, any great teachings, the Father was well-pleased with the Son!

Among other things this indicates that our every day actions are noticed by the Lord. Therefore, like Jesus, it is important that we are faithful in the "little things."

Consequently, the entire earthly life of Jesus provides a pattern for our behavior. We are to follow His example.

What Did Jesus Look Like?

A question that is frequently asked concerns the physical appearance of Jesus Christ. People wonder if the Scripture gives any direct testimony as to what Jesus looked liked physically. The answer is, "No." There is nothing in the Bible that describes the physical characteristics of Jesus. There are, however, a few indirect references that give us some idea of what He looked like. We can make the following observations.

1. HIS APPEARANCE WAS NOT OUTSTANDING

We can surmise from the Scripture that Jesus was not outstanding in His appearance. He was probably of average size for a man living in His day. We can deduce this from the record of His betrayal. Judas Iscariot made a pact to betray Jesus for thirty pieces of silver. The chief priests and religious rulers wanted to be sure they had the right man.

> Judas had told them ahead of time, "Arrest the man I greet with a kiss" (Matthew 26:48 CEV).

If Jesus had been above average in height or had some outstanding physical characteristic, then it is hard to imagine why Judas needed to point Him out. Jesus obviously did not stand out that strikingly in a group of eleven other men.

2. HE WAS MISTAKEN FOR A GARDENER

At His resurrection, Mary Magdalene first thought Jesus was the gardener. We read in John's gospel.

> After she said this, she turned around and saw Jesus standing there. However, she didn't know that it was Jesus. Jesus asked her, "Why are you crying? Who are you looking for?"
>
> Mary thought it was the gardener speaking to her. So she said to him, "Sir, if you carried him away, tell me where you have put him, and I'll remove him" (John 20:14,15 God's Word).

Again, if He had some unmistakable physical characteristic, whether Jesus being very tall or very short, then it would be difficult to imagine Him being mistaken for a gardener. Even though Mary was not expecting a resurrected Christ, any outstanding physical characteristic would probably have been noticed right away. The fact that she did not immediately know Him seems to further indicate that there was nothing extraordinary about His appearance.

3. HE WAS NOT UGLY OR DEFORMED

Some take the prophecy that Isaiah makes of the coming Messiah to indicate He was ugly or deformed. It reads as follows.

> Like a young plant or a root that sprouts in dry ground, the servant grew up obeying the Lord. He wasn't some handsome king. Nothing about the way he looked made him attractive to us (Isaiah 53:2 CEV).

But this prophecy more likely refers to the battered condition of His body while on the cross. It may also be a reference that He was merely average in His looks. It does not necessarily mean that He was somehow deformed in appearance.

Moreover, it does not explain why Jesus had to be singled out of a crowd of people. If He were somehow deformed, there would have been no need for a sign from Judas.

Also the Scripture tells us that little children came to Jesus of their own accord. Usually children are afraid of someone who has a physical deformity because of a natural fear of the unknown. This would further indicate that there was nothing unusual about Jesus' appearance.

In the Old Testament, the sacrificial lamb was to be without spot or blemish. This was a picture of Jesus, the Lamb of God, who was the perfect sacrifice for our sin. Although the perfection of Jesus was spiritual, that is, He did not have any sin, it might also have reference to His physical characteristics. But of this point we cannot be sure. Therefore, we cannot make any definite conclusions.

SOME ANCIENT TESTIMONY TO THE LIKENESS OF JESUS

We have some ancient testimony to the making of a physical likeness of Jesus. They include the following.

1. WAS A STATUE OF JESUS MADE?

There is the testimony of the early church father Eusebius that a statue of Jesus had been made by the woman whom Jesus healed from hemorrhaging. He said that he had seen this statue of Jesus in the city of Caesarea Philippi. The statue was ordered destroyed by order of the anti-Christian Roman Emperor, Julian the Apostate.

2. WAS A PORTRAIT OF JESUS MADE?

There is also ancient testimony that Luke, the author of the third gospel, painted a portrait of Jesus. The early church father Eusebius mentions this as having occurred. Nothing is known as to what happened to this portrait.

3. WHAT ABOUT THE SHROUD OF TURIN?

We also have the mysterious Shroud of Turin, the purported burial cloth of Christ. If this is the actually burial cloth of Jesus, then we have an actual representation of what He looked like. However, the Shroud has not been proven to be the actual burial cloth of the Lord. The subject of the Shroud continues to be an intriguing mystery with experts either arguing for its authenticity or its fraudulent nature.

SCRIPTURE EMPHASIZES THE INWARD CHARACTER NOT THE OUTWARD APPEARANCE

The fact that the New Testament gives us no description of Jesus illustrates a biblical truth. God is more interested in the behavior of a person than how they look on the outside. In the Old Testament, the Lord said the following to the prophet Samuel.

> But the Lord told him, "Samuel, don't think Eliab is the one just because he's tall and handsome. He isn't the one I've chosen. People judge others by what they look like, but I judge people by what is in their hearts" (1 Samuel 16:7 CEV).

No matter what Jesus looked like on the outside, He was certainly the most beautiful Person who has ever existed!

SUMMARY TO QUESTION 12
WHAT DID JESUS LOOK LIKE?

Though Jesus Christ was God Himself who became an actual human being, we do not know what His physical appearance was like. In fact, there are no direct descriptions of Jesus in the Scripture. The Bible is more concerned about who He was as a Person rather than His outer appearance. Hence we have no physical description. However, we can infer that He was not extraordinary in His looks.

At the time of His betrayal, He had to be picked out of a crowd of eleven other men. It is hard to imagine the necessity of Judas pointing Him out if He were a head taller or shorter than the rest of the disciples.

On the day of His resurrection, Mary Magdalene mistook Him for the gardener. Again, if Jesus were in any manner deformed, or exceedingly short or tall, it would not be likely that she did not immediately recognize Him. This is further indication that there was nothing outstanding in His physical appearance.

Interestingly, there are accounts from church historians that likenesses of Jesus were made. We are told that the woman whom Jesus healed from hemorrhaging made a statue of Him.

In addition, Luke, the author of the third gospel, is said to have painted a portrait of Jesus. However, nothing remains of these likenesses.

Some believe that the mysterious shroud of Turin is the actual burial cloth of Christ. If so, then we do have a likeness of Him. However, as intriguing as it is, the shroud has never been proven to be authentic.

Consequently, anything we can know about Jesus' physical appearance is only from inference. This indicates that the outward appearance was not that crucial. What was important was what was on the inside—in His heart. The Bible describes that part of Him as absolute perfection.

QUESTION 13

What Do We Know About Joseph, Jesus' Earthly Father?

Some two thousand years ago, God the Son became a human being in the Person of Jesus Christ. In doing so, the Bible tells us that He had earthly parents. There are some facts that we know about them.

For one thing, we know they were his earthly father was named Joseph. Scripture tells us certain things about this man. It is important that we discover what it says because there are some valuable lessons for us.

1. JOSEPH WAS NOT THE BIOLOGICAL FATHER OF JESUS

To begin with, Joseph was the husband of Mary, the mother of Jesus, but clearly he was not His biological father. The New Testament makes this point quite emphatically. Matthew explains what occurred in this manner.

> The birth of Jesus Christ came about this way: After His mother Mary had been engaged to Joseph, it was discovered before they came together that she was pregnant by the Holy Spirit (Matthew 1:18 HCSB).

Joseph, while the husband of Mary, was not the father of Jesus. Indeed, he discovered Mary was pregnant through the Holy Spirit.

Faced with this dilemma, Joseph thought of divorcing Mary. Scripture says, however, that the angel of the Lord intervened.

> Because Joseph, her husband to be, was a righteous man, and because he did not want to disgrace her, he intended to divorce her privately. When he had contemplated this, an angel of the Lord appeared to him in a dream and said, "Joseph, son of David, do not be afraid to take Mary as your wife, because the child conceived in her is from the Holy Spirit" (Matthew 1:19-20 NET).

The angel told Joseph the source of the pregnancy of Mary—the Holy Spirit. Joseph was then commanded to take Mary as his wife.

The angel also told Joseph what the name of the Son would be, Jesus. Joseph as further informed that this Child would be the Savior of the people of Israel.

> She will give birth to a son and you will name him Jesus, because he will save his people from their sins." This all happened so that what was spoken by the Lord through the prophet would be fulfilled: "*Look! The virgin will conceive and bear a son, and they will call him Emmanuel,*" which means "*God with us*" (Matthew 1:21-23 NET).

The Child of Mary would actually be "God with us." He would be like no other child who has ever lived.

We find that Joseph immediately obeyed the commandment of the angel of the Lord. Matthew writes.

> When Joseph got up from sleeping, he did as the Lord's angel had commanded him. He married her but did not know her intimately until she gave birth to a son. And he named Him Jesus (Matthew 1:24,25 HCSB).

Joseph married Mary, the virgin. Scripture emphasizes that they did not have any intimate relations until after the time Jesus was born.

2. JOSEPH TAKES MARY TO BETHLEHEM WHERE THE CHILD JESUS IS BORN

Scripture says that Joseph brought his pregnant wife Mary to Bethlehem in obedience to the commandment of Caesar. Luke writes.

> In those days a decree went out from Caesar Augustus that the whole empire should be registered. This first registration took place while Quirinius was governing Syria. So everyone went to be registered, each to his own town. And Joseph also went up from the town of Nazareth in Galilee, to Judea, to the city of David, which is called Bethlehem, because he was of the house and family line of David, to be registered along with Mary, who was engaged to him and was pregnant. While they were there, the time came for her to give birth. Then she gave birth to her firstborn Son, and she wrapped Him snugly in cloth and laid Him in a feeding trough—because there was no room for them at the inn (Luke 2:1-6 HCSB).

Since Joseph was a descendant of King David, he had to go to David's city, Bethlehem, to register in accordance with the decree of Caesar.

3. JOSEPH TAKES THE CHILD AND HIS MOTHER TO EGYPT

Joseph is again mentioned after Jesus was born in Bethlehem. King Herod, upon discovering the Messiah had been born, ordered the young male babies in Bethlehem killed.

> After they were gone, an angel of the Lord suddenly appeared to Joseph in a dream, saying, "Get up! Take the child and His mother, flee to Egypt, and stay there until I tell you. For Herod is about to search for the child to destroy Him." So he got up, took the child and His mother during the night, and escaped to Egypt. He stayed there until Herod's death, so that what was spoken by the Lord through the prophet might be fulfilled: Out of Egypt I called My Son (Matthew 2:13-15 HCSB).

The flight to Egypt fulfilled what the Lord had predicted through the prophet Hosea.

4. THE RETURN FROM EGYPT AND THE MOVE TO NAZARETH

The Holy Family eventually returned to Israel from Egypt but moved to Nazareth upon hearing that Archelaus was ruling.

> After Herod was dead, an angel of the Lord appeared in a dream to Joseph in Egypt. The angel said to him, "Get up, take the child and his mother, and go to Israel. Those who tried to kill the child are dead." Joseph got up, took the child and his mother, and went to Israel. But when he heard that Archelaus had succeeded his father Herod as king of Judea, Joseph was afraid to go there. Warned in a dream, he left for Galilee and made his home in a city called Nazareth. So what the prophets had said came true: He will be called a Nazarene (Matthew 2:19-23 God's Word).

In sum, there are not many facts recorded about Joseph in the four gospels. He is mentioned only with respect to the events surrounding Jesus' birth, the flight to Egypt, and return to Galilee. We find that Joseph obeyed the Lord without question during this time.

5. JOSEPH IS LAST HEARD OF WITH THE EPISODE IN THE TEMPLE

The only other reference to Joseph is the episode regarding Jesus teaching at the temple at age twelve. Luke records this.

> And all who heard him were amazed at his understanding and his answers. His parents didn't know what to think. "Son!" his mother said to him. "Why have you done this to us? Your father and I have been frantic, searching for you everywhere." "But why did you need to search?" he asked. "You should have known that I would be in my Father's house." But they didn't understand what he meant (Luke 2:47-50 NLT).

It is interesting to note that Joseph is not mentioned by name in this account—neither is there any record of him saying anything to Jesus. In fact, there are no recorded words of Joseph contained in Scripture.

The account speaks of Jesus' parents. Mary calls Joseph "Jesus' father" however Jesus corrects her when He emphasizes who His real Father is. This is the last we hear of Joseph.

6. JOSEPH WAS NOT AROUND FOR JESUS' PUBLIC MINISTRY

Joseph is not mentioned as being around when Jesus began His public ministry. He is conspicuous by His absence. Almost everyone agrees that he had died before the time Jesus revealed Himself to the world. We know nothing of the circumstances surrounding his death.

What we do know of Joseph, the husband of Mary, is that he was a godly man who unquestioningly obeyed the Lord. We can only imagine how difficult it was for him to hear the whispers about Mary and the Child she bore. It was all the more difficult because he could not tell anyone the real story about what had occurred. That would have to wait until the time the Child grew to be a man. However, Joseph, like so many others, never lived to see the vindication of his wife Mary.

7. HIS DEATH MAY HAVE BEEN INDICATED

There may be an indication in Scripture that Joseph would never live to see Jesus' public ministry. When the newborn Jesus was brought to the temple in Jerusalem, they were met by an elderly man named Simeon. This man had been promised by the Lord that he would not die until he saw God's Messiah. After speaking prophetic words over the Child Jesus, Simeon spoke to Joseph and Mary about their newborn Son.

> So the child's father and mother were amazed at what was said about him. Then Simeon blessed them and said to his mother Mary, "Listen carefully: This child is destined to be the cause of the falling and rising of many in Israel and to

be a sign that will be rejected. Indeed, as a result of him the thoughts of many hearts will be revealed—and a sword will pierce your own soul as well!" (Luke 2:33-35 NET).

Joseph is called the "child's father." However, Luke has already told his readers who was the real Father of Jesus, God Himself. Since Joseph adopted Jesus at His birth, he could rightly be called Jesus' earthly father.

We also discover that Simeon had direct words for Mary, but not for Joseph. He predicted that a sword would pierce Mary's soul concerning Jesus. Among other things, it speaks of Jesus' rejection and crucifixion.

Yet Simeon said nothing about what would happen to Joseph. This may be an indication that Joseph would not be around to see Jesus rejected and crucified by the people whom He came to save. Whatever the case may be, it seems relatively certain that Joseph did not live to see Jesus' public ministry.

In sum, we can say that Joseph was a godly man who was obedient to the Lord. Indeed, he was asked to do a number of difficult things. We find that each and every time the Lord commanded Joseph to do something, he complied with the command. Therefore, Joseph provides a great example to all of us.

SUMMARY TO QUESTION 13
WHAT DO WE KNOW ABOUT JOSEPH, JESUS' EARTHLY FATHER?

We know some details about Jesus' family. The name of His earthly father was Joseph. However, Joseph was not the biological father of Jesus. The Bible makes this as clear as can be.

While engaged to Mary, but before they had any intimate relations, Joseph was told by the angel of the Lord that his wife-to-be was pregnant through the Holy Spirit. She would give birth to a boy whom he was to name "Jesus." Joseph was thus commanded to take Mary as his wife and raise Jesus as his own. He obeyed, and adopted Jesus upon His birth. Interestingly, we have no recorded words of Joseph. Every time he is mentioned with other people, he is never the one doing the speaking.

We find that Joseph was prominent in the accounts surrounding Jesus' birth, the family's flight to Egypt, and their return to the Holy Land. Joseph is also mentioned in the story of the boy Jesus when He was teaching the elders at the temple—though there is no record of him saying anything at this occasion. We know nothing of the circumstances of the death of Joseph.

There may be a hint of his death before the public ministry of Jesus would even begin. When the Child Jesus was brought to the temple in Jerusalem, a man named Simeon held Him in his arms. He specifically told Mary that a sword would pierce "her heart." He said nothing about Joseph. This may indicate that Joseph would not be around when Jesus entered His public ministry.

What we do know is that Mary is referred to on certain occasions during Jesus' ministry but Joseph is nowhere mentioned as being present. It seems that Joseph passed from the scene before the Lord began the work for which He had been called.

We can sum up the life of Joseph by observing his godly behavior. Indeed, each and every time the Lord called upon him to do something, Joseph immediately obeyed.

In addition, Joseph obeyed the command of Caesar to enroll his family in the hometown of his ancestor David. Although it caused hardship on his pregnant wife to make the long journey, it allowed for the prophecy to be fulfilled—the Christ was to be born in Bethlehem. This unquestioned obedience of Joseph is a lesson for all of us.

What Do We Know About Mary, Jesus' Mother?

Mary is one of the most famous characters in all of Scripture. She was the wife of Joseph and the biological mother of Jesus. We know the following things about her.

1. THE ANGEL GABRIEL TOLD HER ABOUT JESUS' MIRACULOUS CONCEPTION

While she was a virgin, the angel Gabriel appeared to Mary and announced the coming birth of Jesus. Luke records the following.

> In the sixth month of Elizabeth's pregnancy, God sent the angel Gabriel to Nazareth, a town in Galilee, to a virgin pledged to be married to a man named Joseph, a descendant of David. The virgin's name was Mary. The angel went to her and said, "Greetings, you who are highly favored! The Lord is with you." Mary was greatly troubled at his words and wondered what kind of greeting this might be. But the angel said to her, "Do not be afraid, Mary; you have found favor with God. You will conceive and give birth to a son, and you are to call him Jesus. He will be great and will be called the Son of the Most High. The Lord God will give him the throne of his father David, and he will reign over Jacob's descendants forever; his kingdom will never end." "How will this

be," Mary asked the angel, "since I am a virgin?" The angel answered, "The Holy Spirit will come on you, and the power of the Most High will overshadow you. So the holy one to be born will be called the Son of God. Even Elizabeth your relative is going to have a child in her old age, and she who was said to be unable to conceive is in her sixth month. For no word from God will ever fail." "I am the Lord's servant," Mary answered. "May your word to me be fulfilled." Then the angel left her (Luke 1:26-38 NIV).

Mary was told that she would supernaturally conceive a Son who would rule forever. She then willingly obeyed the Word of the Lord.

2. MARY PRAISED GOD FOR HIS FAITHFULNESS: THE SONG OF MARY

There is the song of Mary recorded in Luke's gospel (Luke 1:46-55) in which Mary praises God for His faithfulness. Among other things, she said the following.

My soul praises the Lord's greatness! My spirit finds its joy in God, my Savior (Luke 1:46,47 God's Word).

Her Son would also be her Savior.

Mary correctly predicted that she would be called blessed from that time on. The Bible records her saying the following.

Because he has looked favorably on me, his humble servant. "From now on, all people will call me blessed" (Luke 1:48 God's Word).

She was indeed blessed of God.

3. MARY WAS PRESENT AT JESUS' FIRST MIRACLE

At the site of Jesus' first miracle, when He turned water into wine, His mother Mary was present. John records this.

On the third day there was a wedding in Cana of Galilee, and the mother of Jesus was there. Now both Jesus and His disciples were invited to the wedding. And when they ran out of wine, the mother of Jesus said to Him, "They have no wine." Jesus said to her, "Woman, what does your concern have to do with Me? My hour has not yet come." His mother said to the servants, "Whatever He says to you, do *it*" (John 2:1-5 NKJV).

This shows us that Mary realized Jesus' ability to perform a miracle— although He had not performed one up to this point.

4. MARY WAS WITH JESUS' BROTHERS AND SISTERS ON ONE OCCASION

There is a recorded account of Mary being with Jesus' brothers and sisters in an attempt to restrain Jesus and bring Him back home. We read about this in Mark.

When his family heard about it, they went to get him. They said, "He's out of his mind!" (Mark 3:21 God's Word).

The "they" most likely refers to Jesus' own family rather than the crowd. It seems Jesus' entire family thought that He was deluded. This may have included his mother Mary.

This interpretation is reinforced by what we later find in this chapter. We are told that His family attempted to speak to Him on this occasion. Mark further writes.

Then Jesus' mother and brothers arrived. Standing outside, they sent someone in to call him. A crowd was sitting around him, and they told him, "Your mother and brothers are outside looking for you." "Who are my mother and my brothers?" he asked. Then he looked at those seated in a circle around him and said, "Here are my mother and my brothers!" (Mark 3:31-34 NIV).

Jesus emphasized that His real family consisted of those who did the will of God. We know that His brothers did not believe in Him during the time of His earthly ministry. John wrote.

> For not even his own brothers believed in him (John 7:5 NET).

At the very least, we find that Mary's faith was not strong enough to keep His own brothers from wanting to bring Him back home. Whatever the case may be, we discover that Mary, like the rest of us, was an imperfect human being who needed a Savior.

5. MARY WAS PRESENT AT THE CRUCIFIXION

She was present at Jesus' crucifixion. John, alone among the Gospel writers, tells us this. He wrote the following.

> Standing by the cross of Jesus were His mother, His mother's sister, Mary the wife of Clopas, and Mary Magdalene. When Jesus saw His mother and the disciple He loved standing there, He said to His mother, "Woman, here is your son." Then He said to the disciple, "Here is your mother." And from that hour the disciple took her into his home (John 19:25-27 HCSB).

John the Apostle then took Mary into his home.

6. SHE WAS IN THE UPPER ROOM AFTER JESUS' ASCENSION

The last we hear of Mary is with Jesus' disciples in the Upper Room. We read about this in the Book of Acts.

> The apostles had a single purpose as they devoted themselves to prayer. They were joined by some women, including Mary (the mother of Jesus), and they were joined by his brothers (Acts 1:14 God's Word).

Here she is called the "mother of Jesus." After this, there is no mention of Mary in the New Testament. We know nothing with respect to the circumstances of her death.

7. MANY FANCIFUL STORIES AROSE ABOUT MARY

After the New Testament era, many fanciful stories were written about Joseph and Mary. However, the only facts about their lives of which we can be certain are those that are recorded in the New Testament.

8. JESUS REBUKED A WOMAN FOR ATTEMPTING TO PUT MARY ON A PEDESTAL

There is also an incident in the ministry of Christ which teaches us not to elevate Mary to a place where she does not belong. Luke records the following incident.

> As he said these things, a woman in the crowd raised her voice and said to him, "Blessed is the womb that bore you, and the breasts at which you nursed!" But he said, "Blessed rather are those who hear the word of God and keep it" (Luke 11:27,28 ESV).

The New Century Version puts it this way.

As Jesus was saying these things, a woman in the crowd called out to Jesus, "Blessed is the mother who gave birth to you and nursed you."

> But Jesus said, "No, blessed are those who hear the teaching of God and obey it" (Luke 11:27,28 NCV).

This episode teaches us some valuable lessons. To begin with, His response was not insulting to Mary. She was indeed blessed by being the mother of the Lord. Actually, the woman in the crowd was attempting to complement Jesus.

On the other hand, Jesus said that those who heard the Word of God, believed it, and then acted upon it, would have an even greater position than His own mother. At the very least, Jesus' statement to this woman in the crowd should caution us against venerating Mary too highly. Mary was blessed among women but certainly, as the Lord expressed here, she was not blessed "above all women." We need to always keep this in mind.

SUMMARY TO QUESTION 14
WHAT DO WE KNOW ABOUT MARY, JESUS' MOTHER?

We know some details about Jesus' mother Mary. She was married to a man named Joseph. However, the Bible makes it clear that Joseph was not the actual father of Jesus, but adopted Him upon His birth. Jesus was supernaturally conceived by the Holy Spirit.

Indeed, Mary was a virgin when the angel announced to her that she would give birth to the Messiah. While she figures prominently into the birth narrative of Jesus, there are only a few other occasions where she is mentioned.

We find her at the wedding of Cana of Galilee when Jesus turns the water into wine. She suggested that Jesus perform some miracle when the wedding party ran out of wine. While Jesus did perform a miracle, He made it clear that it was to be His miracle—done His way and in His time.

Mary was also with Jesus' brothers when they wished to restrain Him from doing His ministry, as well as bring Him back home. In fact, the Bible says His family thought that He was deluded. It is possible to conclude that Mary too shared this sentiment with Jesus' brothers.

At the very least, she could not restrain her other sons from wanting to bring Jesus back home. Like the rest of us, Mary had her lapses of faith.

However, Mary was there at His crucifixion. She was taken into the home of the Apostle John after the death of Jesus. Her sons, Jesus' brothers, were not with her when Jesus was crucified.

The last mention of Mary in the New Testament is before the Day of Pentecost where she is together with the other disciples. After this, we hear nothing of her.

While many fanciful stories arose about Mary, the only authoritative information which we have about her is found in the New Testament.

From an account that Luke records, we find that Jesus did not encourage the veneration of His mother above other people. While she was blessed by being the mother of Jesus, Scripture never elevates her to a position of superiority. Like the rest of us, she was a sinner who needed a Savior.

Consequently, we should have a balanced view of her. She certainly is "blessed" for being chosen to be the mother of Jesus, there is no doubt about this. On the other hand, we should reject the idea of venerating or elevating her above all others. The Lord, and He alone, deserves our worship!

Did Jesus Have Brothers And Sisters?

The birth of Jesus was the result of a supernatural union between God the Holy Spirit and his mother Mary. Indeed, she was a virgin at the time Jesus was conceived.

There are some who maintain that Mary remained a virgin throughout her entire life. If this were the case, then Jesus would have been an only child. The Scriptures, however, indicate that Jesus did have brothers and sisters.

1. THE TESTIMONY OF MATTHEW: MARY DID NOT REMAIN A VIRGIN

The first testimony that Mary did not remain a virgin can be found in the opening chapter of Matthew. When Joseph had discovered that Mary was going to have a child, he decided to secretly divorce her. He had not had sexual relations with her and knew the child was not his.

But an angel appeared to Joseph in a dream and told him that his wife's pregnancy was through God, the Holy Spirit. Later we are told the following.

> But did not know her intimately until she gave birth to a son. And he named Him Jesus (Matthew 1:25 HCSB).

Matthew 1:25 strongly suggest that Joseph had normal sexual relations with Mary *after* the birth of Jesus. Thus this passage provides a strong argument against any idea of the perpetual virginity of Mary.

JESUS HAD BROTHERS AND SISTERS

Furthermore, Scripture gives testimony to the fact that Joseph and Mary had other children who were brothers and sisters of Jesus. We are told that the brothers of Jesus went along with Him and His mother to Capernaum.

> After this, He went down to Capernaum, together with His mother, His brothers, and His disciples, and they stayed there only a few days (John 2:12 HCSB).

This occurred after they had attended a wedding in Cana of Galilee. Notice that "His brothers" are mentioned as a distinct group from His disciples.

We also read in Matthew about the brothers of Jesus. It says.

> He was still speaking to the crowds when suddenly His mother and brothers were standing outside wanting to speak to Him. Someone told Him, "Look, Your mother and Your brothers are standing outside, wanting to speak to You." But He replied to the one who told Him, "Who is My mother and who are My brothers?" And stretching out His hand toward His disciples, He said, "Here are My mother and My brothers! For whoever does the will of My Father in heaven, that person is My brother and sister and mother" (Matthew 12:46-50 HCSB).

The Bible clearly says that Jesus had brothers and sisters.

2. THE PEOPLE AT NAZARETH ACKNOWLEDGE JESUS' FAMILY

On another occasion, we are told that the people in His hometown of Nazareth became indignant at His claims.

Is not this the carpenter, the son of Mary and brother of James and Joses and Judas and Simon? And are not his sisters here with us? And they took offense at him (Mark 6:3 ESV).

They knew His family well. The crowd mentions four brothers and at least two sisters. Therefore, we learn that Jesus had sisters as well as brothers.

3. JESUS' BROTHERS DID NOT INITIALLY BELIEVE IN HIM

John tells us that during the ministry of Jesus His brothers did not believe in Him. He wrote.

So His brothers said to Him, "Leave here and go to Judea so Your disciples can see Your works that You are doing. For no one does anything in secret while he's seeking public recognition. If You do these things, show Yourself to the world." (For not even His brothers believed in Him.) (John 7:3-5 HCSB).

At that time, His brothers were not believers.

4. HIS BROTHERS BELIEVE IN HIM AFTER HIS RESURRECTION

This all changed after His resurrection from the dead. We are told that Jesus appeared to His brother James. Paul wrote.

After that He was seen by James, then by all the apostles (1 Corinthians 15:7 NKJV).

We also find His brothers, with Jesus' disciples, waiting for the coming of the power of the Holy Spirit on the Day of Pentecost. The Bible says.

They all joined together constantly in prayer, along with the women and Mary the mother of Jesus, and with his brothers (Acts 1:14 NIV).

His brothers, plural, were there. This probably indicates that Jesus made some appearance to them.

5. JAMES BECOMES A LEADER IN THE CHURCH

James became an active leader in the church. Indeed, he was the leader of the church in Jerusalem. In fact, it seems that he presided over a council that was held in Jerusalem. We read about this in the Book of Acts.

> There was no further discussion, and everyone listened as Barnabas and Paul told about the miraculous signs and wonders God had done through them among the Gentiles. When they had finished, James stood and said, "Brothers, listen to me" (Acts 15:12,13 NLT).

Paul mentioned James in one of his letters.

> Three years later I went to visit Peter in Jerusalem and stayed with him for fifteen days. The only other apostle I saw was James, the Lord's brother (Galatians 1:18,19 CEV).

James is called "the Lord's brother."

Paul also called James a "pillar of the church" and compared his authority to that of Peter and John. He wrote to the Galatians.

> In fact, James, Peter, and John, who were known as pillars of the church, recognized the gift God had given me, and they accepted Barnabas and me as their co-workers. They encouraged us to keep preaching to the Gentiles, while they continued their work with the Jews (Galatians 2:9 NLT).

It is generally believed that the New Testament books, James and Jude, were written by two of Jesus' brothers, though neither of them calls themselves Jesus' brother in their introduction. James wrote.

> James, a bondservant of God and of the Lord Jesus Christ, To the twelve tribes which are scattered abroad: Greetings (James 1:1 NKJV).

Jude called himself James' brother.

> From Jude, a servant of Jesus Christ and the brother of James.
> To all who are chosen and loved by God the Father and are
> kept safe by Jesus Christ (Jude 1:1 CEV).

They may have been thinking of Jesus' statement that His mother and brothers and sisters are those who did the will of God—not those who are genetically related to Him.

> Anyone who does the will of my Father in heaven is my
> brother and sister and mother (Matthew 12:50 NLT).

Consequently, the relationship these two had with Jesus, after His resurrection, was based upon their belief in Him—not their blood relationship.

THERE ARE THREE VIEWS AS TO THE IDENTITY OF JESUS' BROTHERS AND SISTERS

Who were these actual brothers and sisters of Jesus? There are three views as to their identities that have become popular. They are as follows.

VIEW 1: THEY WERE YOUNGER BROTHERS AND SISTERS OF JESUS

The first view states that there were children born to Mary and Joseph after Jesus. Hence, the four brothers and two sisters who were mentioned were His younger brothers and sisters (natural half-brothers and sisters).

This is certainly the most normal and simplest way of understanding the totality of the New Testament evidence. We read the following about Jesus birth in Luke.

> She gave birth to her first-born son. She dressed him in baby
> clothes and laid him on a bed of hay, because there was no
> room for them in the inn (Luke 2:7 CEV).

By calling Jesus Mary's "firstborn" seems to demonstrate that she had other children after Him. While the word "firstborn" can mean pre-eminent, it can also mean the "first in time." It all depends upon the context. That Mary and Joseph had their own children after the birth of Jesus is consistent with all the other evidence.

THE ARGUMENT FROM JESUS' KINGSHIP

There is also the argument made that Jesus could not have had older brothers and sisters because of His claim to David's throne. For Jesus to be the legal heir to the throne of David, He had to be the oldest Son. We can explain the situation in this manner.

THE PROMISE TO DAVID

King David was promised that his dynasty would permanently rule over Israel. We read of this in First Chronicles. The Bible says.

> But the Lord said to me: 'You have spilled a great deal of blood and fought many battles. You must not build a temple to honor me, for you have spilled a great deal of blood on the ground before me. Look, you will have a son, who will be a peaceful man. I will give him rest from all his enemies on every side. Indeed, Solomon will be his name; I will give Israel peace and quiet during his reign. He will build a temple to honor me; he will become my son, and I will become his father. I will grant to his dynasty permanent rule over Israel' (1 Chronicles 22:8-10 NET).

The Messiah had to be a descendant of King David, through his son Solomon, to fulfill this prediction.

Matthew begins his gospel by tracing Jesus Christ to King David's family line through his son Solomon.

This is the record of the genealogy of Jesus Christ, the son of David, the son of Abraham. . . David was the father of Solomon (by the wife of Uriah), Solomon the father of Rehoboam (Matthew 1:1,6, 7 NET).

Thus, Jesus Christ could not be the legal King of Israel unless He was the legal Son of Joseph—for those in Joseph's line were heirs to the throne. While Mary was also a descendant of David through David's son Nathan, as we see in Luke's genealogy, this was not the royal line. Thus, Nathan's descendants would have no right to the throne.

Since the line of Joseph was the royal line, Jesus had to have been legally the eldest Son of Joseph. This is why Joseph could not have had children through a previous marriage. Otherwise, the eldest son in that marriage would have been the rightful heir to the throne.

VIEW 2: THEY WERE CHILDREN OF JOSEPH FROM A PREVIOUS MARRIAGE

Some people believe that the brothers and sisters who are mentioned were children of Joseph from a previous marriage (step-brothers and sisters). This would make the four brothers, and at least the two sisters, older than Jesus.

The reason some believe that they were not children of Joseph and Mary is due to the way they are designated in a couple of contexts.

JESUS IS THE SON OF MARY

In Mark 6:3, Jesus is called the "Son of Mary" and is distinguished separately from the brothers who are named, as well as the sisters. However, the fact that He is called Mary's Son may be due to the fact that Joseph, the husband of Mary, was no longer alive. It certainly does not force us to assume that the other brothers and sisters were children of Joseph from a previous marriage.

THEY ARE CALLED JESUS' BROTHERS

In the upper room were "Mary the mother of Jesus, and . . . his brothers" (Acts 1:14). Here they were called His brothers, not her sons. Again, this has led some to speculate that they were sons of Joseph from a previous marriage.

However, this designation could merely be a way of distinguishing them from Jesus' other disciples. It does not necessarily mean they were not the actual children of Mary.

Epiphanius, a fourth century defender of the perpetual virginity of Mary, held the view that these were Joseph's children from a previous marriage. It was also the view held by the ancient scholar Jerome. Modern defenders of this view include the great scholar Joseph Barber Lightfoot.

However, if this were the case we run into the problem of the firstborn son being the lawful heir to the throne. If Joseph had sons older than Jesus, the eldest would be the rightful heir. This is one of the many facts which seem to rule out any possibility that these were half brothers of Jesus through a previous marriage of Joseph.

VIEW 3: THEY WERE COUSINS OF JESUS, NOT BROTHERS AND SISTERS

There has also been the theory that the brothers and sisters who are mentioned were cousins of Jesus—not His actual brothers and sisters. They were the sons of Cleopas who was either a brother or brother-in-law of Joseph.

The support for this argument is the Hebrew and Aramaic use of the term for "brother." In the Old Testament, we find brother used for near relations.

> So Abram said to Lot, "Let's not have any quarreling between
> you and me, or between your herdsmen and mine, for we are
> brothers" (Genesis 13:8 NIV).

Lot was actually Abraham's nephew. We read in the Book of Genesis.

> Abram and his allies recovered everything—the goods that had been taken, Abram's nephew Lot with his possessions, and all the women and other captives (Genesis 14:16 NLT).

This view would allow Jesus to be the firstborn Son of Joseph and the rightful heir to the throne of David. While this view is theoretically possible, there is nothing in Scripture to indicate Jesus' brothers and sisters were actually His cousins.

In addition, there is a Greek word that is specifically used for cousins. In fact, we find that word used in the description of the disciple Mark. We read the following.

> Aristarchus, who is in prison with me, sends you his greetings, and so does Mark, Barnabas's cousin. As you were instructed before, make Mark welcome if he comes your way (Colossians 4:10 NLT).

Therefore, it seems that if the four brothers of Jesus were His cousins, the gospel writers would have used that specific word to make the relationship clear—as is done with respect to Mark and Barnabas.

WHICH SOLUTION IS CORRECT?

While all three solutions have been offered as possibilities, the traditional view is the only option which fits all the biblical facts. Thus, we conclude that Jesus had actual brothers and sisters that were the biological children of Mary and Joseph.

SUMMARY TO QUESTION 15
DID JESUS HAVE BROTHERS AND SISTERS?

The New Testament says that God the Son, Jesus Christ, was born to Mary, the virgin. Though she was married to Joseph, the New Testament makes it clear that Jesus was not the biological Son of Joseph.

However, Joseph adopted Jesus and therefore He was legally the Son of Joseph—though not biologically. Consequently, Jesus had the proper credentials to be the Promised Messiah.

The Scripture also says that Jesus had four brothers and at least two sisters. Exactly how they are related to Him has been a matter of controversy. There have been three popular views in the history of the church. They include the following.

The natural sense in which to take the references is they were His actual younger brothers and sisters—biological children of Joseph and Mary. This is the usual way in which they are understood.

There is something else that needs to be appreciated. Joseph was in royal the line of David. To have the proper credentials to be the promised Messiah, Jesus would have had to have been the oldest Son of Joseph. If He was not, then He would not have been able to claim the title of Messiah. This is another reason to assume that the brothers and sisters of Jesus were born to Joseph and Mary after Jesus had been born.

However, some people believe they were step-brothers and sisters of Jesus from a previous marriage of Joseph. Thus, Joseph was a widower when he married to Mary. The problem with this view is that Jesus would not have been the oldest Son of Joseph, and thus not legally the heir to David's throne.

A third view thinks they were cousins of Jesus. It is argued that the words translated "brothers and sisters" can mean cousins in some contexts. While this view allows Jesus to be the oldest Son of Joseph and Mary, and thus legally in line for the throne, there is no reason to assume that this is what the gospel writers meant when referring to Jesus' brothers and sisters. In fact, there is a specific Greek word for cousins that is used elsewhere in the New Testament. If they were Jesus' cousins, we would expect that word to be used in the four gospels—but it is not.

Therefore, the best view to hold is that these were Jesus' younger brothers and sisters born to Joseph and Mary after His birth. Consequently, Jesus would have had the proper credentials to be the promised Messiah.

Has The Actual Burial Box Of James, Jesus' Brother, Been Found

In October, 2002 a surprising announcement was made that could have major implications for biblical studies. An ossuary, or burial box, from the first century A.D., was found to contain the names of James, Joseph, and Jesus.

The Aramaic inscription on the side of the box can be translated as follows.

> Jacob (James) the son of Joseph brother of Jesus

The obvious question: Is this the same James mentioned in the New Testament that is the brother of Jesus, and the son of Joseph?

THE BURIAL BOX: AN OSSUARY

An ossuary is not the same thing as a grave or tomb. It is a box where the bones of someone who had previously been buried were placed. About a year after a person was buried the bones were dug up and placed in an ossuary. The ossuary does not contain an entire skeleton intact. It only has to be large enough to contain the femur—the longest bone in the human body.

A NUMBER OF IMPORTANT QUESTIONS NEED TO BE ANSWERED

The announcement of the discovery of this ossuary brings up a number of important questions. They include the following.

1. IS IT AUTHENTIC?

The first question that has to be addressed concerns the authenticity of ossuary and the inscription. Is it really a first century receptacle for the bones of a man named James, or is it a fraud. Most experts who have examined the ossuary believe it to be authentic.

2. DOES IT REFER TO THE NEW TESTAMENT CHARACTERS?

If authentic, does it refer to the New Testament characters? Even if this is an authentic first-century ossuary, should we assume that it is from the same James mentioned in the New Testament—the brother of Jesus? While there could have been other men with the name James who had a brother named Jesus and a father named Joseph, the likelihood that it refers to a different James is remote. For one thing, this combination of names would not have been all that widespread.

However, what seems to give strong evidence for its authenticity as being the James of the New Testament is the mention of his brother—Jesus. Only one other ossuary discovered from that time period has the name of the brother of the deceased as well as the father. In every other case, it is only the father who is mentioned. The fact that James is referred to as the brother of Jesus is a strong indication of its identification with James the son of Mary.

IF SEEMINGLY AUTHENTIC, THEN WHAT WOULD IT MEAN?

This brings us to the question of what all of this would mean. To begin with, this would be the first physical evidence of the existence of Jesus, His half-brother James, as well as Joseph the husband of Mary. It is the first inscription from that period in which we find their names.

SOME OBJECTIONS TO ITS AUTHENTICITY

As can be imagined, there have been a number of objections to the claim that this ossuary actually contains the bones of James—the brother of Jesus. They include, but are not limited to, the following.

OBJECTION 1: SCIENCE HAS PROVED THE OSSUARY TO BE A FRAUD

A seemingly fatal objection to the authenticity of the ossuary came soon after it was discovered. A team of experts from Israel examined the burial box and unanimously declared it to be a fraud. They concluded that it was an ancient burial box that had been tampered with in modern times. This, is seems, was the end of the story.

In addition, the man who owned the burial box has been accused of being involved in another "ancient find" that has turned out to be an obvious hoax—a tablet, which was supposedly written eight centuries before Christ. This adds to our suspicion about the genuineness of the burial box.

But not so fast. While the report of these experts seemingly closed the door on the ossuary being authentic, a closer looks shows that the issue had not been resolved.

For one thing, it has been pointed out that the leader of the committee who made the conclusion was an outspoken critic of the ossuary from the beginning. Furthermore, it has been alleged that he persuaded some of members of the committee to agree to this conclusion even though they had their own reservations about declaring the ossuary to be a hoax.

In addition, the scientific conclusions of this Israeli panel have also been disputed by other scientists who have looked at the ossuary. Even after the report of these Israeli experts, they continued to argue for its authenticity.

Thus, the conclusion that was made with such public fanfare, that the ossuary and its inscription was a modern hoax, may not be the last word on the subject. The ossuary may indeed prove to be a fake. However, we should be careful not to assume that the matter is now closed.

OBJECTION 2: IT WAS NOT DISCOVERED BY TRAINED ARCHAEOLOGISTS

The ossuary was not discovered by trained archaeologists in a dig, but rather it was purchased by an Israeli citizen from an antiques dealer. This, it is argued, makes its authenticity suspect.

However, this does not necessarily follow. The Dead Sea Scrolls are in the same category. They were not initially discovered by archaeologists in the field but rather were purchased from a dealer. Nobody doubts their authenticity. While it would have been simpler for all concerned if this ossuary was found in the midst of some sponsored dig, the fact that it came from a private citizen who purchased it from a dealer does not rule out it from being authentic.

OBJECTION 3: THE LETTERING IS FROM TWO DIFFERENT HANDS

Another objection is that the lettering on the ossuary was not written by one writer but two. It is argued that "James the son of Joseph" was written by a different person than the one who wrote "the brother of Jesus." If this is the case, then the authenticity of the ossuary should be seriously questioned.

While this claim has been made, it has not been accepted by most authorities. They argue that the writing consists of one person writing at one time in history.

WHAT WOULD IF MEAN IF AUTHENTIC?

If the ossuary is authentic, then several things would be true. It would mean there is now physical evidence for three New Testament characters—Joseph, Jesus, and James. It would also give further confirmation to the fact that Jesus was considered to be an important figure since His name was on James' burial box.

WHAT SHOULD WE CONCLUDE ABOUT THE AUTHENTICITY OF THIS BURIAL BOX?

As of now, the best that we can say is that the ossuary was possibly the burial box for the bones of James. Unfortunately, because of the way in which it was made public, and the suspicious circumstances around the man who owned the box, there can never be certainty of its authenticity.

Add to this the testimony of the Israeli experts who declared it to be a fraud after scientifically testing it. Doubts will also persist. In addition, it may be discovered some time in the future that the entire episode was fraudulent and no one will argue for its authenticity.

However, as the situation now stands, we have to have some reservations about its genuineness.

This should be a valuable lesson for all of us. Indeed, when news comes of some sensational find about Jesus, or some other biblical character or event, we should be careful to jump to quick conclusions. The right way of approaching these issues is with caution. Eventually the truth of the matter will emerge. Until it does, we should be very careful as to how we embrace such claims.

SUMMARY TO QUESTION 16
HAS THE ACTUAL BURIAL BOX OF JAMES, JESUS' BROTHER, BEEN FOUND?

It is possible that the actual bones of James, or Jacob, the son of Mary and the half brother of Jesus, have been discovered. Much of the evidence seems to indicate that the ossuary is authentic.

In addition, the combination of names makes the identification with the James of the New Testament likely. If authentic, it provides the first physical evidence that Jesus existed.

The objections that have so far been brought forward against the identification are not convincing to everyone. However, because of the object was not discovered in an archaeological dig by reputable scholars, and because of the questionable motives of the Israeli citizen who owned the box, there will always be some degree of doubt concerning its authenticity.

What Historical Facts Do We Know About The Life Of Jesus?

It is important for everyone to understand that there is a central core of truth upon which both believers and unbelievers agree upon concerning the life of Jesus Christ.

From the New Testament we can deduce the following facts about the life and ministry of Jesus of Nazareth.

FACT: JESUS CHRIST EXISTED

Today, no serious scholar doubts the existence of Jesus. The fact that Jesus lived is an established historical fact. Twenty-seven separate documents of the New Testament give firsthand testimony to His existence. There are at least nine different writers who provide this evidence.

Also a number of non-Christian writings mention Jesus. Indeed, both Jewish and Gentile sources testify to His existence. Thus, this issue has been settled.

FACT: JESUS CHRIST CLAIMED TO BE THE SON OF GOD

All evidence that we have about Jesus, from the New Testament as well as from other sources, admits that Jesus claimed a special relationship between Himself and God—that of Sonship. The fact that He made these unique claims about Himself is beyond dispute.

Indeed, the religious rulers used this claim of Jesus as the reason why they sought to put Him to death. We read in the gospel of John.

> The Jews answered him, "We have a law, and according to that law he ought to die because he has made himself the Son of God" (John 19:7 ESV).

The reason they wanted Jesus dead is because of the claims which He made.

FACT: HE PREDICTED HIS CRUCIFIXION AND RESURRECTION

From the gospels we have the clear picture that Jesus predicted His death by crucifixion and resurrection. We read in Matthew's gospel.

> From that time Jesus began to show his disciples that he must go to Jerusalem and suffer many things from the elders and chief priests and scribes, and be killed, and on the third day be raised (Matthew 16:21 ESV).

That these predictions were made is confirmed by the fact that the Jewish religious leaders asked the Romans to place a guard at the tomb. We read in Matthew.

> The next day, that is, after the day of Preparation, the chief priests and the Pharisees gathered before Pilate and said, "Sir, we remember how that impostor said, while he was still alive, 'After three days I will rise.' Therefore order the tomb to be made secure until the third day, lest his disciples go and steal him away and tell the people, 'He has risen from the dead,' and the last fraud will be worse than the first" (Matthew 27:62-64 ESV).

Why would anyone guard the tomb if there had not been some prediction of a resurrection? Again, we are on solid historical footing here.

FACT: JESUS CHRIST WAS CRUCIFIED AND BURIED IN JERUSALEM

The Gospels, as well as the Apostle Paul, unanimously testify that Jesus died by crucifixion in the city of Jerusalem and was then buried.

For example, Paul wrote.

> Now, brothers and sisters, I want to remind you of the gospel I preached to you, which you received and on which you have taken your stand. By this gospel you are saved, if you hold firmly to the word I preached to you. Otherwise, you have believed in vain. For what I received I passed on to you as of first importance: that Christ died for our sins according to the Scriptures, that he was buried, that he was raised on the third day according to the Scriptures (1 Corinthians 15:1-4 NIV).

There is no historical evidence to the contrary from any reliable source. Thus, we can conclude that Jesus was crucified, as well as buried, in Jerusalem.

FACT: THERE WAS AN EMPTY TOMB ON EASTER SUNDAY

Three days after His burial, the tomb of Jesus was empty. If it had been occupied, then the enemies of Christianity would have produced the body. The fact that unbelievers said that the disciples of Jesus had stolen His body testifies that the tomb was empty.

Of course, an empty tomb does not necessarily mean a resurrection but the fact that His tomb was empty is beyond all doubt.

FACT: THE DISCIPLES BELIEVED JESUS APPEARED TO THEM

The disciples of Jesus believed that they had seen Him alive after His death on the cross. They assumed that He had risen from the dead. There is no doubt that this was their belief. The Apostle Paul wrote of these appearances.

And that he appeared to Cephas, and then to the Twelve. After that, he appeared to more than five hundred of the brothers and sisters at the same time, most of whom are still living, though some have fallen asleep. Then he appeared to James, then to all the apostles, and last of all he appeared to me also, as to one abnormally born (1 Corinthians 15:5-8 NIV).

There is no doubt whatsoever that these disciples believed that they had seen Jesus alive after He had died.

FACT: THE DISCIPLES' LIVES WERE TRANSFORMED

There is something else which we know to be true. These same disciples were eventually transformed from cowards to martyrs. Because of the influence of Jesus, the lives of these men were radically altered.

On the night Jesus was betrayed, they all scattered.

In that hour Jesus said to the crowd, "Am I leading a rebellion, that you have come out with swords and clubs to capture me? Every day I sat in the temple courts teaching, and you did not arrest me. But this has all taken place that the writings of the prophets might be fulfilled." Then all the disciples deserted him and fled (Matthew 26:55-56 NIV).

However, less than two months later, they were boldly proclaiming the message of Jesus. We read in the Book of Acts.

Then Peter stood up with the Eleven, raised his voice and addressed the crowd: "Fellow Jews and all of you who live in Jerusalem, let me explain this to you; listen carefully to what I say" (Acts 2:14 NIV).

Peter then preached Jesus Christ to them.

Again, there was no doubt their lives were changed. The question is "what changed them?"

FACT: THE RESURRECTION WAS THEIR MESSAGE

The message of Jesus' band of disciples was that He had risen from the dead. The Book of Acts, as well as the writings of Paul and the other New Testament authors, has the resurrection of Christ as their central message. Of this, there is not the slightest doubt.

FACT: THE MESSAGE WAS FIRST PROCLAIMED IN JERUSALEM

Some fifty days after the death of Jesus Christ, the message of His resurrection was heralded in Jerusalem—the very city where the events took place. His disciples fearlessly proclaimed that Jesus had risen.

On that day, Simon Peter said the following to the crowd which had gathered.

> Men of Israel, hear these words: Jesus of Nazareth, a man attested to you by God with mighty works and wonders and signs that God did through him in your midst, as you yourselves know—this Jesus, delivered up according to the definite plan and foreknowledge of God, you crucified and killed by the hands of lawless men. God raised him up, loosing the pangs of death, because it was not possible for him to be held by it (Acts 2:22-24 ESV).

What makes this all the more important is that they proclaimed this message in the same place where the events of Jesus' final days took place. In other words, they were not afraid of what people would discover when their story was investigated.

FACT: THE CHURCH GREW RAPIDLY

A group of believers in Jesus Christ banded together and became known as the church. The church grew rapidly, based on the belief that Jesus had risen from the dead.

All of the above are solid historical facts that are agreed upon by both believers and nonbelievers alike. There is no reason whatsoever to dispute any of this.

FACT: THE NEW TESTAMENT WAS WRITTEN FROM THE PERSPECTIVE THAT JESUS HAD RISEN

Finally, another historical fact which is not in doubt, is that the New Testament was written from the perspective that Jesus was a miracle worker, that He had claimed to be Israel's Messiah, and that He had risen from the dead.

There is no doubt that the writers believed this about Jesus. The question of course is this: What caused them to believe it? Obviously, something made them believe these things. What was it?

The most logical explanation is the one given in the New Testament. Jesus did all of these things which are attributed to Him. This means that He is everything which He claimed to be.

SUMMARY TO QUESTION 17
WHAT HISTORICAL FACTS DO WE KNOW FOR CERTAIN ABOUT THE LIFE OF JESUS?

There are a number of facts that we are able know about the life and ministry of Jesus Christ. We can summarize the main ones as follows.

First, He existed. There is no really doubt that Jesus was a historical character. Indeed, in the New Testament we have twenty-seven separate documents by nine different writers all of whom testify to Jesus' existence.

Add to this there are Jewish and Gentile sources who, as antagonists, admit that He existed. Consequently, His existence should be beyond all doubt.

Furthermore, Jesus also made some astonishing claims about Himself. All ancient sources agree to this.

We also know that Jesus predicted His crucifixion and resurrection. There would have been no reason to guard Jesus' tomb unless He predicted He would come back from the dead. Consequently, we are on solid historical footing here.

All sources agree that Jesus was crucified and buried in the city of Jerusalem. Again, we are in an area where there is no dispute among the written sources.

It is also an historical fact that Jesus' body was not in the tomb on Easter Sunday. Had the body been still in the tomb, it would have been produced by those who hated Jesus and everything He stood for. Yet they could not produce a body.

We also know that the disciples of Jesus claimed that they saw Jesus alive after He had been dead. There is no doubt about their belief.

Furthermore, their message to the world was that "Jesus has risen from the dead!" The message was first proclaimed in Jerusalem, the place where the events took place. Again, we are dealing with solid historical facts.

The New Testament church experienced rapid growth based upon the belief of the resurrection of Jesus. The swift spread of Christianity is another historical fact.

All of these are known historical facts for believer and unbeliever alike.

Finally, we have a New Testament which was written from the perspective that Jesus Christ lived, performed miracles, fulfilled prophecy, and came back from the dead three days after His death.

There is no doubt whatsoever that the writers of the New Testament believed this to be true. Obviously, something caused them to believe these things about Jesus.

Therefore, some explanation must be given for their belief—an explanation that fits all the historical facts. The only consistent explanation is the one in which they give. Jesus Christ, the man from Galilee, came back from the dead. In doing so, He showed Himself to be both Lord and Savior.

PART TWO

Which Written Records About Jesus Are Trustworthy?
Are The Four Gospels Reliable?

We have discovered that Jesus Christ was indeed an historical character. There are a number of ancient sources that testify to His existence while no ancient source denies He existed. Consequently, the fact that He lived is really beyond all doubt.

However, we need to know more than the fact that Jesus lived. Indeed, it is important that we have reliable records about Him so that we can have a trustworthy account of His life and ministry. Can we have any accurate knowledge of Jesus, or are we left with unreliable evidence about Him?

This section looks into the reliability of the various sources that claim to give us testimony about Jesus' life and ministry. The main sources are the four gospels. They claim to have been written by people who had firsthand knowledge of Jesus' life and ministry. We will examine their claims as well as their reliability.

Apart from the four gospels, there have been other works about the life and ministry of Jesus that have been written. While not everything written about Jesus has survived, there are a few writings that claim to contain information about what He said or what He did.

This section of our book will also examine some of the more popular early writings that claim to give us insight into the life and ministry of Jesus. We will see if any of them can add to our knowledge of Christ.

QUESTION 18

What Are The Main Issues We Face In Determining The Reliability Of The New Testament Account Of Jesus?

There is no doubt that Jesus of Nazareth existed as an historical character. The evidence from the New Testament, as well as other secondary sources, all testify to that fact. No ancient source, even from those who did not believe in Him, denied that He existed. This being the case, we need to know about the reliability of the records that we do have about Him. Can they be trusted?

FIVE QUESTIONS WHICH NEED ANSWERING

As we begin to look at the reliability of the New Testament account about Jesus, there are five basic questions that need to be addressed. We need to have a positive answer to each of these questions if we are to have confidence in the New Testament record.

First, we need to know if the text reads the same way as the New Testament writers originally wrote it. Are we reading what they actually said, or have their words been changed? The text needs to read the same—if we are to have any confidence in the message.

Second, if we do have a correct representation of what they originally wrote, then we ask the question about the desire of the writers to accurately record information about Jesus. In other words, did they attempt to give us an accurate portrayal of Jesus? Did they want us to know the truth about Jesus?

Our third question concerns their ability to do this. Even if they desired to give an accurate account of the words and deeds of Jesus, were they in a position to do so? Could they accomplish the task of giving a reliable portrayal of Christ?

Fourthly, we look at the evidence that we now possess. Does the New Testament, as we now have, demonstrate that the disciples did indeed accurately record the life and ministry of Jesus? Is it an accurate and trustworthy account of what He said and did?

Our fifth question concern other works. Are there any other writings about Jesus and His ministry that are more accurate and trustworthy than the four gospels? If so, do they tell the same story, or do they tell a radically different story?

We will look at each of these questions individually.

1. WAS THE TEXT TRANSMITTED ACCURATELY?

The first issue concerns the text of the four gospels. Have they been transmitted to us in a reliable manner, or have they been changed so much that we cannot really tell what they originally said?

The evidence is clear: we can be assured that what we read today is the same thing as the New Testament writers originally wrote. The science of textual criticism demonstrates beyond all doubt that the text we read today has not been changed, or altered in any way, throughout the history of its transmission.

We have gone into this issue in much detail in other books we have written. For example, in our book titled "Ten Reasons to Trust the Bible" we detail the evidence for the reliability of the New Testament text. We do the same thing in even more detail in our book "The Case For Christianity." We refer to these books for the documentation of the trustworthiness of the biblical text.

2. WERE THE WRITERS INTERESTED IN RECORDING RELIABLE INFORMATION ABOUT JESUS

Once we have determined that the text has been reliably transmitted, we need to know if the writers of the four gospels wanted to truthfully inform us about Jesus' life and ministry. Is there evidence that the writers of the New Testament wished to convey information about Jesus that was accurate and true? The answer is an unqualified yes. For example, Luke tells us that his goal was to tell his readers the exact truth about Jesus.

> Having carefully investigated all of these accounts from the beginning, I have decided to write a careful summary for you, to reassure you of the truth of all you were taught (Luke 1:3,4 NLT).

Luke wanted to reassure his readers of the truth of the things they had been taught about Jesus. Indeed, they had not believed in myths or fables.

The Apostle John wrote his gospel so that people would believe in Jesus as the promised Messiah. He stated his purpose in this manner.

> Now Jesus did many other signs in the presence of the disciples, which are not written in this book; but these are written so that you may believe that Jesus is the Christ, the Son of God, and that by believing you may have life in his name (John 20:30,31 ESV).

John tells us the exact purpose of writing of his gospel—it is to create belief in Jesus as the Messiah, the Christ.

This brings up an important point. The gospel writers were not disinterested academic historians who were merely recording a number of ancient historical events for the benefit of future generations. They wrote to convince people that Jesus was the Messiah, the Christ. They are telling us that He is the only One who could save people from the sins. The message of Jesus is the hope for all humanity. Therefore, the writers had an awesome responsibility to present the story correctly.

Because of their desire to tell the truth about Jesus, and the importance of whom He was and what He said and did, we have every reason to believe that the writers of the gospels desired to give us a correct understanding of Him and His ministry.

3. WERE THE WRITERS IN A POSITION TO RECORD RELIABLE INFORMATION ABOUT JESUS?

The evidence is that the New Testament writers intended to give the world a reliable portrait of Jesus. This being the case, do we find that they were in a position to accomplish their goal? Could they give us a true picture of what Jesus said and did?

We find that the writers of the four gospels were certainly in a position to accomplish their desired purpose. They were either eyewitnesses to the events they recorded, or they recorded eyewitness testimony. John would later write.

> That which was from the beginning, which we have heard, which we have seen with our eyes, which we looked upon and have touched with our hands, concerning the word of life—the life was made manifest, and we have seen it, and testify to it and proclaim to you the eternal life, which was with the Father and was made manifest to us—that which we have seen and heard we proclaim also to you, so that you too may have fellowship with us; and indeed our fellowship is with the Father and with his Son Jesus Christ (1 John 1-3 ESV).

They wrote about what they heard, what they saw, and what they touched. In other words, they were there!

4. DID THE WRITERS RECORD RELIABLE INFORMATION ABOUT JESUS?

The writers of the New Testament claim to give us reliable information about Jesus. Furthermore, they were in a position to do so.

Next, we look at how the information written in the New Testament matches up with the facts as we know them.

Again we emphasize that the people were there at the scene. John, the writer of the fourth gospel, emphasized that he was an eyewitness to the events. For example, he was there at the exact moment when Jesus died on the cross. He writes.

> When they came to Jesus, they did not break His legs since they saw that He was already dead. (But one of the soldiers pierced His side with a spear, and at once blood and water came out. He who saw this has testified so that you also may believe. His testimony is true, and he knows he is telling the truth (John 19:33-35 HCSB).

This testimony of John demonstrates that he was an eyewitness to Jesus' death. He saw the blood and water come out separately when the spear was thrust into Jesus' side. This is a perfect explanation, in simple terms, of what happens after a person dies. We find that the blood escapes into the pericardium—the sac around the heart. After standing there for a short time, the blood then separates into serum (water) and clots (the red corpuscles, or blood).

Therefore, if a dead person was thrust through with a spear, and the spear entered the pericardium, "blood and water" would flow out separately just as John stated.

In sum, we have an example here of a New Testament writer who was not only accurate, he was minutely accurate in his description. Examples such as this can be multiplied.

The evidence leads us to conclude that the New Testament writers did indeed leave the world with a truthful account of Jesus. All the evidence indicates that the writers correctly recorded the events of Jesus' life and ministry.

5. ARE THERE ANY OTHER RELIABLE FIRST-HAND SOURCES?

Finally, we consider the possibility of older, better sources to reconstruct the life of Jesus. Do they exist? If so, should we use them instead of the four gospels to discover who Jesus is, as well as what He said?

There are indeed other sources about the life and ministry of Jesus that do tell a different story about Him. However, there is no evidence whatsoever that they should be given priority over the New Testament. There are two reasons why this is so.

First, they were written much later than the New Testament. They are not a firsthand account of who Jesus claimed to be, or the deeds which He did. These works were not composed by people who were there. Consequently, they cannot give us any reliable information about Jesus.

Second, they have all the earmarks of legends. Indeed, when one reads these accounts it becomes apparent that we are in the realm of legend, not fact. In other words, their accounts are really not believable

In sum, we can confidently go to the four gospels, and to them alone, for trustworthy information about Jesus. Indeed, we have every reason to believe that these four documents give us reliable information about His life and ministry.

SUMMARY TO QUESTION 18
WHAT ARE THE MAIN ISSUES WE FACE IN DETERMINING THE RELIABILITY OF THE NEW TESTAMENT ACCOUNT OF JESUS?

There is no doubt that Jesus Christ existed. This being the case, we need to know where we can go to derive reliable information about His life and ministry.

We know that the only firsthand testimony for Jesus is found in the New Testament. Thus, it is important that we examine the reliability of the information which is contained within its pages. Five questions need to be answered.

First, we need to be assured that the written text has been transmitted to us accurately. We find that this is what happened. Indeed, the evidence leads us to believe that it says the same thing today as what was originally written. Consequently, we can work with the text which we now have because we know it accurately reflects the original words of the New Testament writers.

Second, we need to know that the New Testament writers were attempting to write an accurate portrayal of the life and ministry of Jesus. From their writings, we can determine that this was their goal. Indeed, it was their stated goal—to tell us exactly what happened in the life of Jesus. In other words, they tell us that they were not making up stories or fables.

Third, it is important that they were in a position to accomplish their purpose. We find this to be true also. The writers were either eyewitnesses of the events in Jesus' life, or recorded eyewitness testimony. Therefore, their words carry the authority of someone who was there.

Fourthly, we need to know if what they said matches up with known reality. In other words, do the people, places, and events correspond to what we know about the times in which Jesus lived? Again, the evidence available to us is that the New Testament writers did indeed write an accurate account of what Jesus said and did. From all the evidence we possess, we find that their accounts match up to known history and known facts.

Finally, we must be assured that the New Testament is the best and most reliable source of the life and ministry of Jesus. From a look at all the facts, we discover that the New Testament is the only source of reliable information about Jesus. All other sources are later and do not contain firsthand information.

Therefore, we conclude that it is to the New Testament that we must go to find out who Jesus was, and what He did. It is the only firsthand reliable source which we have.

Who Wrote
The Four Gospels?

The only firsthand testimony that we have about the life and teachings of Jesus comes from the four Gospels. Who were the people that wrote these books? The traditional authorship is credited to Matthew, Mark, Luke, and John. How do we know this is correct? What evidence is there that these people actually wrote the gospels that are attributed to them?

THERE ARE THREE BASIS REASONS TO TRUST THE TRADITIONAL AUTHORSHIP

There are three basic reasons why we believe these men wrote the four gospels that bear their names rather than these documents being composed by someone else. We can state these reasons as follows.

REASON 1: THERE IS UNANIMOUS TRADITION AS TO THE AUTHORSHIP OF THE FOUR GOSPELS

To begin with, in the ancient world, the four gospels are unanimously attributed to Matthew, Mark, Luke and John. Indeed, there are no other candidates. Every ancient source that deals with their authorship attributes the gospels to these men and to nobody else.

There is something else which needs to be stressed. The four gospels were accepted as authoritative works on the life of Christ by the first generation of Christians. Since the gospels were received as trustworthy at an early date, it is unlikely, if not impossible to believe, that the original authors of these works would have been forgotten.

To quickly command acceptance from the people who believed in Jesus, it had to have an author that was known to them, as well as from someone who could be accepted as an authoritative source. Each of the four gospels met these criteria.

REASON 2: THREE OF THE FOUR ARE UNLIKELY AUTHORS

The authors of our four gospels would not have been the obvious choices to write the accounts of the life of Christ. Only one of these four men (John) was a prominent character in the New Testament. The others, though mentioned, were relatively minor figures.

Why then attribute a book to Matthew, Mark, and Luke if they were not the authors? The evidence for these unlikely choices is as follows.

MATTHEW

Matthew was a former tax collector, a customs official, who was a minor figure in the New Testament. He records his own conversion as follows.

> As Jesus went on from there, He saw a man named Matthew
> sitting at the tax office, and He said to him, "Follow Me!" So
> he got up and followed Him (Matthew 9:9 HCSB).

The fact that Matthew had collected taxes for Rome, from his own people, would have made him hated by the Jews. Apart from Judas, he would have been the least loved of the twelve apostles.

Why attribute a gospel to him if you are targeting Jewish people with the good news about Jesus? He would seem to be the least likely candidate among the twelve. Yet, the first gospel has always been attributed to him.

MARK

Mark, or John Mark, was not one of the Twelve. He is identified in the New Testament in a number of passages. For example, it was at the house of his mother Mary, which some members of the early church gathered to pray.

> So, when he had considered this, he came to the house of Mary, the mother of John whose surname was Mark, where many were gathered together praying (Acts 12:12 NKJV).

Therefore, the family of Mark was intimately involved with the work of the early church.

We also find that Mark went along with Barnabas and Saul on a missionary voyage. We read about this in the Book of Acts. It says.

> And Barnabas and Saul returned to Jerusalem after they had completed their relief mission, on which they took John Mark (Acts 12:25 HCSB).

Therefore, this man was a missionary.

However, at a later time, Paul refused to take him along on another missionary journey. We read about this later in the Book of Acts.

> Barnabas wanted to take along John Mark. But Paul did not think it appropriate to take along this man who had deserted them in Pamphylia and had not gone on with them to the work. There was such a sharp disagreement that they parted company, and Barnabas took Mark with him and sailed off to Cyprus (Acts 15:37-39 HCSB).

With such an unfavorable description of Mark by Paul, it is remarkable one of the four gospels would have been attributed to him—had he not written it.

Fortunately, Paul eventually found Mark useful in the ministry. In his last letter, Paul wrote to Timothy and mentioned John Mark.

> Luke alone is with me. Get Mark and bring him with you, for he is very useful to me for ministry (2 Timothy 4:11 ESV).

Interestingly, we find two of the four gospel writers, Mark and Luke, with Paul while he was in prison awaiting execution.

LUKE

This brings us to our next unlikely candidate, Luke. He was not one of the Twelve. Rather, he was seemingly a Gentile and a traveling companion of Paul. He is only mentioned by name three times in the New Testament.

In the final part of his letter to the Colossians, Paul calls him the beloved physician. We read.

> Luke, the beloved physician, and Demas, greet you (Colossians 4:14 KJV).

He was obviously familiar to the people of Colosse.

Paul also mentions Luke in his letter to Philemon—along with others who send their greetings. He wrote the following.

> Epaphras is also here in jail for being a follower of Christ Jesus. He sends his greetings, and so do Mark, Aristarchus, Demas, and Luke, who work together with me (Philemon 23,24 CEV).

Luke was seemingly familiar to Philemon.

Yet this is all that we know of him. Once again, we find a minor character in the New Testament unanimously attributed to having a gospel written by him.

The unanimous attestation of these unlikely authors is another strong reason for accepting the traditional view that they penned their respective gospels.

Other names, prominent in the New Testament, would have carried more weight with people than these three relatively unknown individuals. Again, there is no reason to attribute authorship to these people had they not written these works. None whatsoever.

REASON 3: THE DOCUMENTS WERE IDENTIFIED BY TAGS

The early preservation of the name of the author is another consideration. It was a common literary practice during the time of Christ to preserve the name of the author of a written work. Scrolls with written text on both sides had tags glued to them (called a *sittybos* in Greek) that insured the preservation of the author's name. They were attached in such a way that a person could see who authored the scroll without unrolling it. This is similar to the function of the spine on our modern books—one does not have to open the book to find out who wrote it.

With four different written gospels circulating, there needed to be a way to distinguish them from each other. The term "gospel" would not be enough—seeing that there was more than one circulating.

Therefore, the church had to preserve the name of each gospel writer at an early date. The tag on the outside of the scroll would accomplish that purpose. It would read in Greek, "Gospel According to Matthew" or "Gospel According to Mark," etc.

The fact that this happened is clear in that there are no variations in the titles of the gospels. Every source is unanimous that Matthew wrote Matthew, Mark wrote Mark, Luke penned his gospel, and John wrote his.

These three reasons, the unanimous testimony of the church, the unlikely authorship of these men, and the early identification of the document, all present a strong case for the traditional authorship of the gospels.

THE APOCRYPHAL GOSPELS CLAIMED AUTHORSHIP FROM MORE PROMINENT FIGURES

There is one more thing that should be mentioned. The apocryphal, or false gospels, that sprang up later in the history of the church did use the names of more important New Testament characters as their supposed author.

Thus, we have such works as the "Gospel of Mary," the "Gospel of Peter," and the "Gospel of James."

Peter, Mary, and James, Jesus' brother, are three of the most prominent figures in the New Testament and certain writings were attributed to them after the time of the apostles.

While nobody seriously believes these people wrote the so-called "gospels" credited to them, it does point out their prominence, as well as providing further confirmation that the gospels we now have, Matthew, Mark, Luke, and John, come from the people traditionally believed to have written them.

SUMMARY TO QUESTION 19
WHO WROTE THE FOUR GOSPELS?

Four separate works known as gospels have recorded the life and ministry of Jesus Christ for us. The traditional authorship is credited to Matthew, Mark, Luke, and John. There are three basic reasons why we believe these men wrote the four gospels. We can list them as follows.

First, the early church was unanimous in their testimony as to the individual authorship of each gospel. There are no other candidates! This evidence alone should answer the question.

However, there is more. Apart from John, the writers of the various gospels were obscure figures in the history of the church. Matthew was a hated tax collector. He certainly would not have been an expected author of one of the gospels.

Mark was once considered to be unprofitable by the Apostle Paul for the ministry. One would think a person like that would not have been chosen to write one of the gospels. Yet, he was.

The author of the third gospel, Luke, was not even Jewish. Like Matthew and Mark, he is an obscure New Testament character.

So we have the obvious question. Why attribute these sacred writings to them if they did not compose them? There is no reason to credit these men with the writing of the gospels had they not done it.

At the time of Christ, it was also a practice to glue a tag on the outside of a scroll. The purpose of this tag was to identify the individual author of the work. This practice made certain the name of the author was retained. This is another factor that should cause us to be certain the correct authors have been identified.

Add to this the fact that people like Peter, Mary, and James had gospels attributed to them later in the church. They were much more prominent figures than Matthew, Mark and Luke. Again, why attribute a gospel to a lesser known figure when there were more prominent individuals who would seem more likely candidates?

The evidence is clear and convincing. The traditional belief that Matthew, Mark, Luke, and John wrote the four gospels is the only view that fits the known facts.

Were The Writers Of The Four Gospels Qualified To Write About Jesus?

The four gospel writers are unanimously attributed to Matthew, Mark, Luke, and John. There are no other candidates. While only John was a prominent character in the New Testament, each had excellent credentials to be in a position to know the facts about Jesus' ministry and to record them correctly. The evidence is as follows.

MATTHEW

The writer of the first gospel originally bore the name Levi but was also named, or possibly renamed, Matthew (gift of God). We know that he was the son of Alphaeus. Luke wrote.

> After these things He [Jesus] went out and saw a tax collector named Levi, sitting at the tax office. And He said to him, "Follow Me" (Luke 5:27 NKJV).

Matthew was a member of the Twelve. These were Jesus' inner circle of trusted disciples. Consequently, he would have had access to Jesus' private statements as well as His public ones.

Before Jesus called him to the ministry, his job was that of a hated tax collector, or customs official. This position would have made him an ideal candidate for writing this gospel for the following reasons.

1. A tax collector would be fluent in Greek.

2. He would also be literate—he could read and write.

3. He would be used to keeping records.

4. He most likely would be able to write in short-hand. Therefore, he could have been a note-taker at Jesus teachings.

5. If Levi was a tribal name, he would have known about scribal tradition and be familiar with temple practices.

6. He would have been a well-educated scribe in the secular sense of the term.

7. There is something else about the tax collector position that would make Matthew a particularly good candidate to be a writer of one of the accounts of the life of Jesus. Being a tax collector, he would be familiar with all types of fraud and deceit. He would be more distrustful than most people. This would make him very cautious about trusting the word of someone.

Therefore, his eyewitness testimony to the words and deeds of Jesus carries considerable weight. He would have written only the things that he knew were true.

Therefore, for a number of reasons, Matthew turns out to be an excellent candidate to record events in the life and ministry of Jesus. He would be in a position to write to Jews about how Jesus fulfilled the Old Testament promises regarding the coming Messiah.

MARK

Mark was also in a unique position to write about Jesus. He was not one of the Twelve Apostles. Therefore, he was not personally in a position to report on what Jesus said and did. However, his gospel contained the preaching of a person who could do exactly this—Simon

Peter. In fact, we are told by ancient sources that Mark was basically a stenographer or recorder of the words of Simon Peter.

Therefore, we have Mark recording the things Simon Peter taught about the life and ministry of Jesus. In fact, there is hardly any incident related in Mark's gospel where Simon Peter was not present. In addition, the recording of minute detail shows that we have the testimony of an eyewitness.

LUKE

Luke, the writer of the third gospel, stated the purpose of his account in the preface. He explained it as follows.

> Many people have tried to tell the story of what God has done among us. They wrote what we had been told by the ones who were there in the beginning and saw what happened. So I made a careful study of everything and then decided to write and tell you exactly what took place. Honorable Theophilus, I have done this to let you know the truth about what you have heard (Luke 1:1-4 CEV).

This statement of Luke tells us, at least, the following things.

1. Luke may not have been an eyewitness to the events he recorded.

2. But he, like those before him, made careful use of the eyewitness accounts.

3. Luke had access to other narratives, possibly written documents like his own.

4. Luke felt the need for a further account of the life and ministry of Jesus.

5. His account is orderly.

6. He had full knowledge of the events he recorded.

7. His ultimate aim is truth.

Luke wanted to make certain that the truthfulness of Jesus' ministry was properly written. This was his stated aim. His main audience consisted of non-Jews, or Gentiles. While Matthew directed his gospel toward Jewish people, Luke wrote to those who had little, if no, knowledge of the customs of the Jews.

JOHN

The author of the fourth gospel, John, was one of the twelve. Consequently, he was an eyewitness to the events in the life of Christ. At the end of the Gospel of John, we find these words.

> This disciple is the one who told all of this. He wrote it, and
> we know he is telling the truth (John 21:24 CEV).

As an eyewitness, John would certainly be in a position to correctly state the facts about who Jesus was, and exactly what He said and did. Indeed, he was there.

EACH OF THEM WAS QUALIFIED TO WRITE ABOUT JESUS

Consequently, each of the four gospel writers was in an excellent position to write about the life and ministry of Jesus. They desired to give us an accurate portrait of Christ, and they were certainly in a position to fulfill that desire. Therefore, there is every reason to trust what they said.

SUMMARY TO QUESTION 20
WERE THE WRITERS OF THE FOUR GOSPELS QUALIFIED TO WRITE ABOUT JESUS?

The life and ministry of Jesus Christ has come down to us in four written documents known as gospels. Traditionally, they have been attributed to Matthew, Mark, Luke and John. There is every reason to believe that they were the actual authors of these documents.

Indeed, we find that each of the four gospels writers was in a position to write an historically accurate account of the life and ministry of Jesus Christ. We can sum up their credentials as follows.

Matthew, the writer of the first gospel, was one of the Jesus' Twelve disciples. This means that he was with the Lord for the three years of His public ministry. Consequently, he basically saw and heard everything that Jesus publicly said and did, as well as hearing His private words.

Furthermore, his credentials were excellent. As a tax collector he would have been fluent in the Greek language. He would also have been able to read and write. Matthew would also be used to keeping records—likely writing them in short-hand. Therefore, he could have taken notes when Jesus taught.

While Mark was not an eyewitness, he recorded the story of Simon Peter who himself was an eyewitness. In fact, there are excellent reasons to believe that Mark recorded Peter's sermons "word for word." If so, then we have another eyewitness account of Jesus' life and ministry.

Luke wrote his account of Jesus after exhaustive historical investigation with the firsthand sources. In his prologue, he states that his aim is to tell the exact truth concerning Jesus. There is every reason to believe that he met his stated purpose.

The fourth gospel writer, John, was not only a member of the Twelve, he was also a member of Jesus' most inner circle. Along with Peter, John was a leader in the early church. He was with Jesus in certain situations where the Lord took along only three or four disciples. Again, we have someone who was in an authoritative position to write to us about the Lord.

Consequently, when we examine all of the evidence, we discover that we have four excellent, independent sources to the life and ministry of Jesus. Therefore, we can be confident that we have a trustworthy account of the things our Lord said and did.

When Were The
Four Gospels Written?

It is important to know when the four gospels were written. Were they composed close to the time of the events in Jesus' life or were they written long after things transpired? Can we know which one was written first?

The evidence shows that the four Gospels were written in a relatively short time after the death and resurrection of Jesus Christ. Examining the internal evidence of the New Testament itself can make this plain. The data are as follows.

THE CITY OF JERUSALEM AND THE TEMPLE WERE STILL STANDING WHEN THE GOSPELS WERE WRITTEN

The first three Gospels, and possibly also the fourth, were apparently written while the city of Jerusalem was still standing. This can be determined as follows.

Each of the first three Gospels contains predictions by Jesus concerning the destruction of Jerusalem and the temple (Matthew 24; Mark 13; Luke 21), but none records the fulfillment. We know that Titus the Roman destroyed the city and temple in A.D. 70.

Hence, the composition of the first three Gospels most likely occurred sometime before this event—otherwise their destruction would have been recorded. The fact that no fulfillment of Jesus' prophecy is given to us is a strong indication that these works were composed before the city and temple were destroyed.

THE BOOK OF ACTS GIVES A CLUE TO THE DATE OF THE GOSPELS

The Book of Acts also provides us with a clue as to when the gospels were written. Acts records the highlights in the life and ministry of the Apostle Paul. The book concludes with Paul at Rome awaiting trial before Caesar. It says.

> And Paul dwelt two whole years in his own hired house, and received all that came in unto him, Preaching the kingdom of God, and teaching those things which concern the Lord Jesus Christ, with all confidence, no man forbidding him (Acts 28:30-31 KJV).

The New Living Translation reads.

> For the next two years, Paul lived in his own rented house. He welcomed all who visited him, proclaiming the Kingdom of God with all boldness and teaching about the Lord Jesus Christ. And no one tried to stop him (Acts 28:30-31 NLT).

The inference is that Acts was written while Paul was still alive—seeing his death is not recorded. Since there is good evidence that Paul died in the Neronian persecution about A.D. 67, the Book of Acts can most likely be dated approximately A.D. 62.

LUKE'S GOSPEL WAS WRITTEN EARLIER THAN ACTS

If Acts were written about A.D. 62, then this helps us date the four gospels. The Book of Acts is the second half of a treatise written by Luke to a man named Theophilus. Since we know that the gospel of Luke was written before the Book of Acts, we can then date the Gospel of Luke sometime around A.D. 60, or before.

THE BROTHER WHO WAS WELL-KNOWN MAY HAVE BEEN LUKE

There may be further evidence for an early date for Luke's gospel. Paul wrote of a brother who was well-known among the churches for the gospel.

> And we are sending along with him the brother who is praised by all the churches for his service to the gospel (2 Corinthians 8:18 NIV).

There is ancient testimony that this refers to Luke and his written gospel. If this is speaking of Luke, and the gospel he composed, then we have it well-known in the mid-fifties of the first century.

MATTHEW, OR MARK, MAY HAVE BEEN A SOURCE FOR LUKE

In his prologue, Luke tells us that he used sources to compose his gospel. This could include written sources.

> Now many have undertaken to compile an account of the things that have been fulfilled among us, like the accounts passed on to us by those who were eyewitnesses and servants of the word from the beginning. So it seemed good to me as well, because I have followed all things carefully from the beginning, to write an orderly account for you, most excellent Theophilus, so that you may know for certain the things you were taught (Luke 1:1-4 NET).

This passage may contain a reference that he used the Gospel of Mark as a written source.

John Mark is called a "minister" or "servant" by Luke in Acts 13:5 (the Greek word *huparetas*). In 1:2, Luke says he derived the information for his gospel from those who were "eyewitnesses" and "ministers" of the word. The term translated "minister" is the same Greek word *huparetas* that described Mark. Therefore, it is possible that this could be a reference to Mark as one of his written sources.

There is also something else that should be considered. There is much material that is common to both Matthew and Luke that is not found in the Gospel of Mark. Since the unanimous teaching of the church is that Matthew was the first gospel written, it is likely that Luke used Matthew as one of his sources.

MATTHEW WAS ALWAYS BELIEVED TO HAVE BEEN WRITTEN FIRST

This brings us to our next point. According to the unanimous testimony of the early church Matthew was the first gospel written. The church father Eusebius places the date of Matthew's gospel in A.D. 41. If the ancient testimony is true, and there is no reason to doubt it, then we have a third independent source about the life of Christ written during the eyewitness period.

JOHN WAS AN EYEWITNESS TO THE EVENTS

The Gospel of John is usually assumed to have been the last of the four gospels composed. John testified that he was an eyewitness to the events that he recorded. He said.

> Now Jesus did many other signs in the presence of the disciples, which are not written in this book; but these are written so that you may believe that Jesus is the Christ, the Son of God, and that by believing you may have life in his name (John 20:30-31 ESV)

The New Living Translation puts it this way.

> Jesus' disciples saw him do many other miraculous signs besides the ones recorded in this book. But these are written so that you may believe that Jesus is the Messiah, the Son of God, and that by believing in him you will have life (John 20:30:31 NLT).

John also wrote.

> This is the disciple who is bearing witness about these things, and who has written these things, and we know that his testimony is true (John 21:24 ESV).

It is clear that John claimed to have been present when the events in the life of Jesus transpired. He was there.

THERE IS INTERNAL EVIDENCE OF AN EARLY DATE FOR JOHN

There is also internal evidence that John himself wrote before A.D. 70. We read the following description of Jerusalem in the fifth chapter of John.

> Now there is in Jerusalem by the Sheep Gate a pool called Bethesda in Aramaic, which has five covered walkways (John 5:2 NET).

John describes the sheep gate as still standing at the time he wrote. He could not have made this statement after A.D. 70 because there was no sheep gate. The sheep gate was destroyed in the year A.D. 70, along with the rest of the city of Jerusalem. The logical implication is that John wrote his gospel before the city of Jerusalem was destroyed.

CONCLUSION: THERE IS EVIDENCE FOR AN EARLY DATE FOR THE FOUR GOSPELS

When all the historical and textual evidence is amassed, it becomes clear that the four gospels were composed at a very early date either by eyewitnesses, or those who recorded eyewitness testimony. Therefore, we have every reason to trust what they wrote.

SUMMARY TO QUESTION 21
WHEN WERE THE FOUR GOSPELS WRITTEN?

One of the important questions with respect to the four gospels concerns the date of their composition. All things considered, the closer they were to the time when these events occurred the better chance of their story being reliable.

When all the evidence is in, it reveals that the four gospels were written soon after the events they recorded. An examination of the Matthew, Mark and Luke reveals that each gospel has Jesus predicting the destruction of the city of Jerusalem as well as the temple. However, none of these writings records the fulfillment.

Since the city and temple were both destroyed in the year A.D. 70, there is good reason to believe that these three gospels were written before this destruction took place. Otherwise we would expect the writers to record the fulfillment of this important prediction which Jesus made.

The same is true with the Gospel of John. It is written from the perspective of the city of Jerusalem still standing. If this is the case, then it would make all four gospels having been written during the period when eyewitnesses, both friendly and unfriendly, were still alive.

There is also possible evidence from the Book of Acts as to the early date of the gospels. Acts is the second part of two books written by Luke. There is internal evidence from Acts that it should be dated before the death of Paul. If this is true, then it was composed before A.D. 67-68 when Paul died. Since Luke's gospel was written before Acts, that would place it in the early 60's of the first century, or earlier.

Add to this that Luke may have used Mark as a written source. This would give us an earlier date for Mark. Luke tells us that he used sources to compose his gospel. There is the belief that one of them was the Gospel of Mark. Of course, if this is true, then Mark had to have been composed before Luke's gospel.

Finally, the early church unanimously believed Matthew was the first gospel written. His gospel could have been written within ten years of the death and resurrection of Jesus. This places the writing of the first three gospels within thirty years of the resurrection of Jesus.

Therefore, each of them would have been composed during the eyewitness period—a time where people who had witnessed the events, both friendly and unfriendly, were still alive.

In sum, between the lack of the recording of the destruction of Jerusalem and the temple, as well as working back from the end of the Book of Acts, we have internal evidence from the New Testament that the gospels were composed fairly soon after Jesus' death and resurrection. All of this gives further testimony to their reliability.

QUESTION 22

Why Are There Four Gospels?

Is there something special about the number four when it comes to the gospels? Could there have been more or less gospels written? Why do we have four authoritative gospels? There are a number of key points which we need to make.

EACH GOSPEL WAS WRITTEN FOR A DISTINCT PURPOSE

It is important that we understand these writings and what they are trying to accomplish. The Gospels are neither biographies of the life of Jesus Christ nor are they a disinterested record of certain events in His life. Each writer wants the reader to know the truth about Jesus and become a disciple. To accomplish this purpose, each Gospel is aimed at a certain audience and each writer is selective of the events he includes. The evidence is as follows.

MATTHEW

The Gospel according to Matthew is aimed primarily at the Jew—the person familiar with the Old Testament. Jesus is portrayed as Israel's Messiah, the King of the Jews. Matthew records how the promises God made in the Old Testament, with regard to the Messiah, are fulfilled in Jesus.

Matthew begins his book by stating the family tree of Jesus.

Jesus Christ came from the family of King David and also from the family of Abraham (Matthew 1:1 CEV).

This genealogy demonstrates that Jesus is the rightful heir to the kingdom that was promised to King David and his descendants. Consequently, it sets the tone for the book. The remainder of the book emphasizes that Jesus has the credentials to be Israel's Messiah.

THE FIRST BELIEVERS WERE JEWS

There is something else that must be considered. In the first few years of the church, all the believers were Jews. According to the Book of Acts, thousands of people converted to belief in Jesus in the few weeks after Jesus' resurrection and ascension into heaven. These people needed to be taught. The Bible says that this occurred immediately.

They were devoting themselves to the apostles' teaching and to fellowship, to the breaking of bread and to prayer (Acts 2:42 NET).

From the beginning, they were taught about Jesus. We should not assume this only included oral instruction. The apostles stayed in Jerusalem during the first few years but believers came and went through the city. They would have wanted, as well as needed, some permanent form of instruction. The Gospel of Matthew, directed at the Jews, would have met this need. Thus, there is every reason to believe that Matthew wrote his gospel at a very early date.

MARK

Mark, on the other hand, is not writing to the Jew, or to those who are familiar with the Old Testament. His audience is basically those people in the Roman Empire who are unfamiliar with the religion of the Jews. Consequently, Mark's gospel does not start with the birth of Jesus—or any family tree that demonstrates Jesus as a fulfillment of Old Testament prophecy. It starts, rather, with the beginning of Jesus' ministry. It says.

This is the good news about Jesus Christ, the Son of God (Mark 1:1 CEV).

Mark's is a gospel of action. Jesus is portrayed as the servant of the Lord. Indeed, Christ is doing the job that God has sent Him to do. Therefore, the emphasis is on doing, and Mark shows that Jesus got the job done. Consequently, Mark's gospel, though the shortest of the four gospels, records more miracles of Jesus than Matthew, Luke, or John.

LUKE

Luke was written to those more intellectually minded. He states his purpose in the book's prologue when he wrote the following.

> Many have undertaken to compile a narrative about the events that have been fulfilled among us, just as the original eyewitnesses and servants of the word handed them down to us. It also seemed good to me, since I have carefully investigated everything from the very first, to write to you in orderly sequence, most honorable Theophilus (Luke 1:1-3 HCSB).

Luke is not writing as an eyewitness, but as one who is recording eyewitness testimony. His portrayal of Jesus is as the perfect man. Hence, he focuses on those events in Jesus' life that stress His humanity. The Greeks in their art and literature were always looking for the perfect human. The Gospel of Luke reveals that man—Jesus of Nazareth.

JOHN

John, the writer of the fourth gospel, was an eyewitness to the life of Jesus. The things he recorded were for the purpose of establishing the fact that Jesus was the eternal God who became a human being. John wanted his readers to exercise faith toward Jesus. In fact, he explained the purpose of his gospel in this manner.

> Jesus did many other miraculous signs in the presence of his disciples, which are not recorded in this book. But these are

written that you may believe that Jesus is the Christ, the Son
of God, and that by believing you may have life in his name
(John 20:30,31 NIV).

When John states his purpose, he also states that he is selective in what
he has recorded. Indeed, Jesus did many more things than what we find
recorded in the gospels. In fact, we have only a fraction of the words
Jesus spoke, or the deeds that He did. At the end of his gospel, John
again stresses that he only chose to record certain events in the life of
Jesus.

> This is the disciple who testifies about these things and has
> written these things, and we know that his testimony is
> true. There are many other things that Jesus did. If every
> one of them were written down, I suppose the whole world
> would not have room for the books that would be written
> (John 21:24,25 NET).

Consequently, while John is telling us everything we need to know
about the life and ministry of Jesus, he also indicates that there is so
much more which could be said.

Therefore, from the four gospels, we have four different authors, from
four different perspectives, writing to four different audiences. Each
of them looks at the life and ministry of Jesus from their own unique
vantage point.

SUMMARY TO QUESTION 22
WHY ARE THERE FOUR GOSPELS?

The four authoritative gospels which have come down to us were written to cover four aspects of the life and ministry of Jesus. We find that
each gospel writer wrote from a different point of view to a different
audience. Thus, they each looked at the character of Jesus from different angles. Therefore, the number four arises from the four different
perspectives we have been given about Christ's life and ministry.

Matthew was written primarily to the Jews. In this gospel, Jesus is pictured as the king of the Jews, the promised Messiah. The emphasis is on His fulfilling the promises found in the Old Testament. Since the first believers were Jews, Matthew was the first gospel which was composed. All ancient sources are unanimous in saying this.

On the other hand, Mark had the Roman world in mind. He pictures Jesus as the One who can do the work God sent Him to do. Though it is the shortest of the gospels, it records more miracles of Jesus than do any of the other writers. While Matthew met the needs of the Jews, Mark showed the Romans that Jesus was a Man of action. In other words, He accomplished those things which He was set out to do.

Luke emphasizes the humanity of Jesus. In their art and literature, the Greeks were looking for a perfect man. However, everyone fell short of perfection. Now the perfect human being has arrived on the scene—Jesus of Nazareth. Consequently, the human aspect of Jesus receives special emphasis in this gospel.

Finally, we have the gospel of John. We find that the King which Matthew portrayed, the Servant of the Lord which Mark wrote about, and the perfect Man whom Luke spoke of, was actually Almighty God who became this human being.

While the first three gospels do record a number of things which shows that Jesus was more than a mere Man, the gospel of John makes His identity clear. He is the Creator, the One who had been God for all eternity. As God, He came to our earth to show humanity what God is like—as well as to die for the sins of the world.

In sum, the gospels are not intended to be a history or biography of the life of Christ in the modern sense of the term. Each author is selective in what he portrays. Jesus did many more things than the Gospels record—as John himself testified.

Consequently, when the Gospels are compared with each other, we get an overall portrait of Jesus. He was God from all eternity that came down to earth as the perfect man. He was the Messiah of Israel, the King of the Jews—the One who did the job that God sent Him to do. This is the testimony of the four Gospels.

QUESTION 23

Why Should We Trust The New Testament Account Of Jesus' Life? Weren't They Biased?

The story of Jesus as recorded in the New Testament is miraculous. There is no doubt about this. From His birth through His resurrection from the dead, Jesus Christ is portrayed as someone who is from heaven. He is the eternal God who came down to earth and became a human being.

The existence of Jesus Christ is beyond question. However, this is not the issue here. Granted that He did exist, could the New Testament story be only a legend? Is it possible that what we have in the New Testament is a fabrication or exaggeration of what actually occurred? After all, those who wrote about Him were admittedly biased. They believed He was the promised Messiah and they wrote with the purpose of convincing others. Does this not make their report suspect?

A number of points need to be made about this all-important question of the bias of the New Testament writers with respect to what they wrote about Jesus.

1. THEY WERE EYEWITNESSES TO THE EVENTS OF JESUS

There are several problems with the view that the New Testament is an exaggeration of the deeds of Jesus. First, we have the testimony of the disciples of Jesus. They contended that Christ did these miraculous deeds in their presence. The Apostle John wrote.

> He who saw this has testified so that you also may believe. His testimony is true, and he knows he is telling the truth (John 19:35 HCSB).

Notice that John is emphasizing the fact that he was there! What he has written is from the perspective of an eyewitness. Nobody told him about these things. Rather he saw them for himself.

Simon Peter, another eyewitness to the life and ministry of Jesus, made it clear that the disciples knew the difference between myth and reality.

> For we were not making up clever stories when we told you about the power of our Lord Jesus Christ and his coming again. We have seen his majestic splendor with our own eyes (2 Peter 1:16 NLT).

Here again we have the emphasis that the events in the life of Jesus were seen by His disciples. With their own eyes they saw the miracles, as well as seeing the risen Christ three days after He was put to death.

Indeed, it is the united testimony of the New Testament that Jesus performed miracles in front of multitudes of people—which included His own disciples. These same disciples are the ones who gave us the New Testament record of His life and ministry. The Gospel writers, Matthew and John, were two of the Twelve. Hence they were eyewitnesses to the events. Mark and Luke recorded eyewitness testimonies.

Consequently, we have the words of individuals who were with Jesus and who witnessed these miraculous events firsthand. They are not passing down a story to us that they had been told. They were there! Each of them independently testifies to the truth.

2. THEY REALIZED THE IMPORTANCE OF THE ISSUES

There is something else which we must take into consideration. The disciples of Jesus Christ realized the importance of the issues they were dealing with. The matters in which they were writing about were of eternal importance. Eternal destinies, including their own, would be determined by how a person viewed Jesus. Therefore, we would expect them to take the utmost care to be as accurate and precise as possible.

3. THEY WOULD HAVE BEEN ALL THE MORE DESIROUS TO WRITE THE TRUTH

Because of the importance of the issue, that the eternal destiny of human beings was based upon the words and deeds of Jesus, these gospel writers would have been all the more desirous to tell the truth. Indeed, they would have exercised exceptional care to make certain they accurately recorded what Jesus said, as well as what He did. They would not be careless with the facts.

In fact, Luke in his prologue tells that that his goal was to relate the precise truth about Jesus. He wanted his readers to know exactly what occurred.

> Many have undertaken to compile a narrative about the events that have been fulfilled among us, just as the original eyewitnesses and servants of the word handed them down to us. It also seemed good to me, since I have carefully investigated everything from the very first, to write to you in orderly sequence, most honorable Theophilus, so that you may know the certainty of the things about which you have been instructed (Luke 1:1-4 HCSB).

Note that Luke wanted his readers to know "the certainty of things," "the exact truth" about what really took place in Jesus' life and ministry.

In the same manner, the Apostle John emphasized that he wrote that which he knew to be true. We read the following words at the end of his gospel.

This is the disciple who testifies to these things and who wrote them down. We know that his testimony is true (John 21:24 HCSB).

Consequently, it is the claim of the gospel writers that they are telling the truth.

4. AN EYEWITNESS IS NOT DISBELIEVED BECAUSE OF BIASES

Another point needs to be made. We cannot disregard their testimony merely because they were believers and wanted to convince others to believe in Jesus. If this is the case, then we cannot accept the testimony of any person, on any issue, who is trying to convince others of what they believe to be true.

In every case, when people are writing for an expressed purpose, we have to weigh and evaluate the evidence. We consider the facts and then make a decision based upon these facts. We do not rule the possibility that they are telling the truth before examining the facts.

5. INITIALLY THEY WERE UNBELIEVERS OF JESUS' RESURRECTION

We need to make one last point concerning this question. It is the testimony of Jesus' disciples that they were the first unbelievers of His resurrection! On Easter Sunday, the women, who had come back from Jesus' tomb, told them that He had risen from the dead. Luke writes about their response.

But these words seemed like nonsense to them, and they did not believe the women (Luke 24:11 CEV).

It was only after they saw the risen Christ, with their own eyes, that the disciples became believers in His resurrection. Therefore, what convinced them was the evidence—it was not some desire to believe what someone else had told them.

Consequently, the often-stated objection, "We cannot accept the disciples report of Jesus because they were biased," is neither the rational thing nor proper thing to do.

Yes, these people were trying to convince others about Jesus. In fact, they tell us that this is their purpose. But this is not the issue. The key question is this: "Do they give us a correct report of what He said and did?" We will discover that this is exactly what they have done.

SUMMARY TO QUESTION 23
WHY SHOULD WE TRUST THE FOUR GOSPEL WRITERS ACCOUNT OF JESUS' LIFE? WEREN'T THEY BIASED?

There are those who object to the New Testament portrayal of Jesus as being truthful because of the source of the testimony. Since the writers were believers in Him, their testimony is assumed to be untruthful and untrustworthy. It is claimed that they are not "objective" sources.

However, to say the New Testament portrait of Jesus was an invention, or exaggeration, does not fit the evidence. The fact that they were His disciples is not the issue. The real issue is this: "Did they tell the truth?" This is the question which must be answered. The evidence is as follows.

To begin with, the testimony we have from the New Testament is from firsthand sources. The disciples recorded what they personally heard and saw. They were eyewitnesses—they were there! This is extremely important to understand.

Therefore, what we have are not second-hand accounts from people who heard stories others told about Jesus. On the contrary, these disciples saw Jesus' miracles with their own eyes and heard His teachings with their own ears. In other words, they are either giving their own eyewitness testimony, or recording the testimonies of eyewitnesses.

In addition, these writers realized the eternal importance of the matters in which they wrote about. Indeed, the destiny of everyone, including their own, depended upon a correct view of Jesus.

Consequently, we would expect them to take the most meticulous care in recording the things Christ said, and the deeds which He did. They knew what was at stake.

Furthermore, Luke emphasizes that his goal in writing his gospel is to tell the exact truth about Jesus. The fact that this is the stated intention of the author should, at the very least, give him the benefit of the doubt when examining his account.

Finally, the idea that the gospels should not be believed because they were written by Jesus' disciples is absurd. We do not reject the eyewitness testimony of people merely because of what they believe about something. We let the facts speak for themselves.

Again we stress the point: it was the appearance of the risen Christ which caused them to believe that He had risen from the dead. Indeed, they were the first people who denied the resurrection took place—the first unbelievers of the story! It was only after they had seen the risen Jesus with their own eyes, and then touched Him, that they became believers.

In sum, there is every reason to accept the New Testament account of Jesus' life and ministry because the sources we have in the four gospels are reliable. We can trust what they have written about Him.

QUESTION 24

Could The Message Of Jesus Have Been Changed By His Own Disciples?

Jesus was crucified, and rose from the dead, in the year A.D. 33. Is it possible that the message of Jesus, as well as the events in His life, were radically changed by Jesus followers before they were committed to writing? How do we know what was written in the four gospels accurately reflects the things Jesus actually said and did? Could they have either knowingly or unknowingly changed the truth about Jesus?

ACCUSATION: THE REAL MESSAGE OF JESUS WAS CHANGED BY HIS DISCIPLES

Those who claim the gospels do not reflect Jesus actual words and deeds usually argue in one of two ways. There are those who think the disciples exaggerated Jesus' story—they were well-meaning but over enthusiastic.

Others believe there was a conspiracy to cover-up exactly what Jesus said and did. In other words, they knew the stories they told were not true but they told them anyway.

Whatever the case may be, the accusation is as follows: what we have in the New Testament is not what Jesus really said, and not what Jesus really did. Key facts have been either omitted or altered. This is the accusation.

OPTION 1: SOME CLAIM JESUS' DISCIPLES EXAGGERATED THE STORY

Many people who reject the gospel accounts believe the disciples exaggerated what Jesus said and did. They do not necessarily believe that their intentions were evil. Supposedly these men were so impressed with Jesus, and missed Him so much after His death, that they began to exaggerate the stories about Him. They turned Jesus into something He was not—a miracle-working Savior who was God Himself.

As the theory is usually stated, this took some time to occur. The gospels are assumed to have been composed many years after Jesus' life and ministry. Indeed, it is often contended that the earliest of the gospels, Mark, was not written until some forty years after Jesus' death. It was during this period that the stories about Him became exaggerated.

OPTION 2: SOME CLAIM THERE WAS A CONSPIRACY

There have also been a number of conspiracy theories. These theories do not think the disciples of Jesus merely changed His message through exaggeration. Instead, they assert that Jesus' disciples, for whatever motivation, hid the real story of Jesus from the world. In other words, there was a deliberate attempt to deceive the people. Of course, those who believe that this is what happened think that *they* have unearthed the real story of Jesus.

RESPONSE: COULD THE MESSAGE HAVE BEEN CHANGED?

Could the real message of Jesus have been changed or hidden from the world? What do the facts really say? The evidence is as follows.

1. THE PERIOD OF ORAL TRANSMISSION WAS SHORT

To begin with, the period of oral transmission was a short span of time. In fact, there was not nearly enough time for the words and deeds of Jesus to be changed. Eyewitnesses, both friendly and unfriendly, were still alive when the gospels were composed.

Furthermore, legends take at least two full generations to develop. This is because eyewitnesses would still be alive in the first generation and there would be people in the second generation who had heard the eyewitness testimony for themselves.

It is only during a third generation when legends could develop without any control of eyewitnesses, or people who heard the eyewitnesses firsthand. Even assuming a late date for the gospels, we are still in this period of time where people would have known the true story of what took place.

2. THEY LIVED IN A MEMORY CULTURE

There is something else. In the world that Jesus lived people relied on their memory much more than we do today. The culture in which Jesus' lived was a memory culture. The spoken word was extremely important. People were trained to listen carefully and memorize.

Furthermore, the people were used to memorizing the sayings and teachings of famous teachers. It has been noted that the teachings of Jesus lend themselves to easy memorization. Consequently, we find the authors of the four gospels composing their works in such a way that would be easy for memorization.

For example, even a modern English version of the Sermon on the Mount, or the Lord's Prayer, reveals an obvious pattern of rhythm and sentences that have a parallel structure. This would have made these teachings easy to memorize.

In addition, memorization also seems to have played a part in selecting an apostle to replace Judas. After the death of Judas, and Jesus' ascension into heaven, a twelfth apostle had to be chosen. How they chose his successor is revealed to us in the Book of Acts where we find the following discussion.

In the book of Psalms it says, "Leave his house empty, and don't let anyone live there." It also says, "Let someone else have his job." So we need someone else to help us tell others that Jesus has been raised from death. He must also be one of the men who was with us from the very beginning. He must have been with us from the time the Lord Jesus was baptized by John until the day he was taken to heaven (Acts 1:20-22 CEV).

The candidate had to have been someone who was with Jesus from the very beginning. In other words, he heard everything that Jesus taught. This would imply that this disciple had memorized Jesus' words.

3. THEY TELL THE SAME STORY

From the first statement until the last, everything that the New Testament writers record about Jesus testifies to His supernatural ability. They all agree that Jesus performed miracles in their presence. The four gospels tell the same basic story about Jesus.

Luke, for example, tells us that he was interested in "the truth."

Most honorable Theophilus: Many people have written accounts about the events that took place among us. They used as their source material the reports circulating among us from the early disciples and other eyewitnesses of what God has done in fulfillment of his promises. Having carefully investigated all of these accounts from the beginning, I have decided to write a careful summary for you, to reassure you of the truth of all you were taught (Luke 1:1-4 NLT).

He tells the same basic story as the other writers. As we compare them, we find that they are in harmony with each other.

4. THE WRITERS DEALT HONESTLY WITH THE FACTS

We also find that the gospel writers give an honest portrayal of the facts. We can cite the following examples of the writers telling the truth—ugly as it was on occasions.

EXAMPLE 1: THE DISCIPLES ARGUED WHO WAS THE GREATEST AMONG THEM

On the night of Jesus' betrayal, after He revealed that one of them would betray Him, the disciples immediately started arguing who was the greatest among them! We read Jesus saying the following.

> The one who will betray me is here at the table with me! The Son of Man will die in the way that has been decided for him, but it will be terrible for the one who betrays him! Then the apostles started arguing about who would ever do such a thing. The apostles got into an argument about which one of them was the greatest (Luke 22:21-24 CEV).

Their insensitivity to Jesus is astounding! Their Lord has just revealed to them the fact that one of them will betray Him and that He will go to His death. Yet, all they could think about was themselves.

EXAMPLE 2: JESUS WAS BETRAYED BY ONE OF HIS OWN DISCIPLES

Matthew records the story of Judas, one of Jesus' own disciples that He Himself had chosen, as betraying Him. We read the following account of what transpired at Gethsemane.

> And suddenly while he was still speaking, Judas, one of the Twelve, appeared, and with him a large number of men armed with swords and clubs, sent by the chief priests and elders of the people. Now the traitor had arranged a sign with them saying, 'The one I kiss, he is the man. Arrest him.' While He was still speaking, Judas, one of the Twelve, suddenly arrived. A large mob, with swords and clubs, was with him from the

chief priests and elders of the people. His betrayer had given them a sign: "The One I kiss, He's the One; arrest Him!" So he went right up to Jesus and said, "Greetings, Rabbi!"—and kissed Him. Friend," Jesus asked him, "why have you come?" Then they came up, took hold of Jesus, and arrested Him. At that moment one of those with Jesus reached out his hand and drew his sword. He struck the high priest's slave and cut off his ear. Then Jesus told him, "Put your sword back in place because all who take up a sword will perish by a sword" (Matthew 26:47-52 HCSB).

Jesus personally chose Judas, yet, Judas betrayed Him. This detail was not necessary to record but it was recorded nevertheless.

EXAMPLE 3: ALL OF JESUS' DISCIPLES ABANDONED HIM AT HIS ARREST

The New Testament also records that all of Jesus' disciples abandoned Him when He was arrested. We read the following in Matthew.

At that moment Jesus said to the crowd, "Have you come out with swords and clubs to arrest me like you would an outlaw? Day after day I sat teaching in the temple courts, yet you did not arrest me. But this has happened so that the scriptures of the prophets would be fulfilled." Then all the disciples left him and fled (Matthew 26:55,56 NET).

There is no reason to make the disciples out to be cowards if they were not. These men were the leaders in the early church.

EXAMPLE 4: PETER, THE LEADER OF THE GROUP, DENIED KNOWING JESUS

The gospels also record Peter denying, or disowning, Jesus on three separate occasions. Matthew records what occurred after Jesus was arrested.

Then they spit in his face and hit him with their fists. Others slapped him and said, "You think you are the Messiah! So tell us who hit you!" While Peter was sitting out in the courtyard, a servant girl came up to him and said, "You were with Jesus from Galilee." But in front of everyone Peter said, "That isn't so! I don't know what you are talking about!" When Peter had gone out to the gate, another servant girl saw him and said to some people there, "This man was with Jesus from Nazareth." Again Peter denied it, and this time he swore, "I don't even know that man!" A little while later some people standing there walked over to Peter and said, "We know that you are one of them. We can tell it because you talk like someone from Galilee." Peter began to curse and swear, "I don't know that man!" Right then a rooster crowed, and Peter remembered that Jesus had said, "Before a rooster crows, you will say three times that you don't know me." Then Peter went out and cried hard. (Matthew 26:69-75 CEV).

Here is the embarrassing story for Peter that was forever memorialized in the gospels. This man, who earlier that night had said that he would die for Jesus, later said that he did not know the man.

EXAMPLE 5: THE DISCIPLES WERE THE FIRST UNBELIEVERS OF THE RESURRECTION STORY

Luke tells us that the disciples were the first unbelievers of Jesus' resurrection. In fact, he tells us they thought the stories they heard from the women were nothing but nonsense. Luke writes.

> But these words seemed like nonsense to them, and they did not believe the women (Luke 24:11 CEV).

This hardly speaks of their great faith. There is more.

EXAMPLE 6: THOMAS DID NOT BELIEVE THE INITIAL REPORTS OF THE DISCIPLES

In our next example, we find that Thomas, one of the Twelve, did not believe when he first heard the reports of the risen Jesus by the other apostles. John writes.

Thomas, one of the twelve apostles, who was called Didymus, wasn't with them when Jesus came. The other disciples told him, "We've seen the Lord." Thomas told them, "I refuse to believe this unless I see the nail marks in his hands, put my fingers into them, and put my hand into his side." A week later Jesus' disciples were again in the house, and Thomas was with them. Even though the doors were locked, Jesus stood among them and said, "Peace be with you!" Then Jesus said to Thomas, "Put your finger here, and look at my hands. Take your hand, and put it into my side. Stop doubting, and believe." Thomas responded to Jesus, "My Lord and my God!" Jesus said to Thomas, "You believe because you've seen me. Blessed are those who haven't seen me but believe (John 20:24-29 God's Word).

In sum, what we find from the New Testament is no desire on the part of Jesus' disciples to make themselves into some type of heroes. To the contrary, they honestly record their lack of understanding of Jesus on certain occasions, the betrayal of Jesus by one of their own, their abandonment of Jesus when He was arrested, and the denial of Jesus by Peter.

In addition, they also tell us that they were the first people to disbelieve the resurrection story! Thus, what we find here is a straightforward account of what truly happened. It is certainly not some attempt to portray themselves in the best possible manner.

5. THE EARLY ENEMIES OF CHRISTIANITY DID NOT DENY THE GOSPEL ACCOUNTS

One important point concerns the response of the early enemies of Christianity to the message of Jesus. They did not deny that Jesus worked miracles. On the contrary, they tried to explain away the events. We find an example of this in Mathew's gospel. We read.

Then they brought him a demon-possessed man who was blind and mute, and Jesus healed him, so that he could both talk and see. All the people were astonished and said, "Could this be the Son of David?" But when the Pharisees heard this, they said, "It is only by Beelzebub, the prince of demons, that this fellow drives out demons" (Matthew 12:22-24 NIV).

The religious leaders, instead of denying Jesus' miracles, actually attributed them to the power of Beelzebul.

Finally, if the New Testament account of Jesus was merely an invention or exaggeration, then why didn't His enemies say so? Those who hated Christ would have denied His miracles—if they could have. Yet they attempted to explain His miraculous character by attributing His works to the power of Satan.

Rather than deny that Jesus was a miracle worker, His enemies tried to say His power was demonic. In doing so, they too, admitted that He performed these wonderful deeds.

We find the same thing with those who lived after the time of Jesus. They never denied His existence. In fact, they never denied that He was a miracle worker. They attempted to give alternative explanations to the miraculous deeds of Jesus that differed from the explanation of the New Testament.

THE GOSPELS WERE WRITTEN SOON AFTER THE EVENTS

There is one other point. The evidence indicates that the gospels were written soon after the events. Matthew, for example, could have been composed as early as ten years after Jesus' death, resurrection, and ascension.

Each of the four gospels was composed in the eyewitness period where people who knew the events, both friendly and unfriendly, could evaluate what they had written.

Thus, with respect to the gospel writers, there was no time, as well as no desire, to change the message of their Lord. None whatsoever.

THE TESTIMONY OF PAUL

One final matter, that is often overlooked in this discussion, is the testimony of Saul of Tarsus—the man who became the Apostle Paul. He wrote a number of letters which became part of the New Testament. From all accounts, his death seems to have taken place somewhere in the 60's of the first century. Of course, this means that his letters were all composed before that time.

In his letters, he confirms many of the facts recorded in the four gospels. Indeed, from Paul we have the testimony of Jesus' identity, that He was a miracle-worker who claimed to be God the Son. Paul also testifies that Jesus died for the sins of the world, and of most importance, Christ came back from the dead three days after His death.

Like the four gospels, his letters were written during the time when eyewitnesses to the events were still alive. Consequently, we have another early source confirming the testimony of Matthew, Mark, Luke and John.

CONCLUSION: THE NEW TESTAMENT PROVIDES THE TRUE ACCOUNT OF JESUS

Therefore, when all the evidence is considered, we should conclude that the New Testament does give us an accurate account of Jesus' words and deeds. The historical facts make it plain that what we have in the New Testament is the historical truth about Jesus. There is no evidence of exaggeration, myth, or some type of conspiracy.

SUMMARY TO QUESTION 24
COULD THE MESSAGE OF JESUS HAVE BEEN CHANGED BY HIS OWN DISCIPLES?

Those who reject the testimony of the gospels, with respect to what Jesus said and did, usually argue against their truthfulness in one of two ways.

One way is to assume the accounts of Jesus became exaggerated. As the stories about Him were told and retold, He was transformed from a simple teacher to a miracle-working Savior. Those who take this position assume the gospels were written some fifty years after Jesus' life. During this time of oral transmission, the stories became exaggerated. While well-meaning, the ultimate writers of the four gospels made Jesus out to be someone whom He was not.

Others do not believe what occurred was so innocent. Indeed, they believe there was a conscious conspiracy to re-write the truth about Jesus. Whatever the case may be, it is assumed that the end result, the four gospels, do not accurately reflect the words and deeds of Jesus.

While there have been those who have argued that the message of Jesus was changed by His disciples before it was finally put into writing, the evidence does not show this.

To begin with, the period of transmitting the message orally was a short period of time. Indeed, there was not enough time for the changes to occur.

In addition, the culture in which the words and deeds of Jesus were transmitted was a culture that was used to accurately remembering what famous people said and did.

We also find that the New Testament writers tell the same basic story about the life of Jesus. While differing in incidental details, the main points remain the same.

In addition, these writers honestly deal with the facts. There is not an attempt to cover up, or fail to report their own faults. In fact, they tell us that they constantly failed.

Indeed, we have the record of the betrayal of Jesus by one of His own disciples, the testimony that all of them abandoned Him on the night which He was betrayed, and the fact that the leader, Peter, denied even knowing Jesus. On Easter Sunday morning, when reports of the resurrection were first given to them by certain women, we find that they did not believe them! Thus, what we find is honest reporting.

There is also the fact that the early enemies of the Christian faith never denied Jesus' miraculous deeds. Even the later unbelievers never denied Jesus' existence or the fact that He was a miracle worker. While they tried to explain away His miracles, they never denied them.

Furthermore, there is much available evidence which shows the gospels were written soon after the events took place—there was not enough time to change the message.

Finally, there is the testimony of Paul. All of his letters were written within a thirty to thirty-five-year period after Jesus' death. He confirms the main facts of the gospel accounts. This provides further testimony to the reliability of their message.

Therefore, the evidence leads us conclude that the gospels accounts have not been changed but rather reflect the true account of what Jesus said and did.

Could The Church Have Conspired To Hide The Real Message Of Jesus? (Holy Blood, Holy Grail, The DaVinci Code)

Over the years a number of people have claimed that the church conspired to cover-up the real story of Jesus. In recent times, two books written on the subject have gained wide popularity: "Holy Blood, Holy Grail" and "The DaVinci Code."

Is there any evidence that the church was actually involved in a cover-up of the events surrounding the life of Jesus? What do these books allege to tell us? Since these claims have achieved popularity in the secular world it is important that we have some type of response to them. We can make the following observations about this issue.

HOLY BLOOD, HOLY GRAIL

In 1982, the book "Holy Blood Holy Grail" was released. This book became a best-seller. Basically, it details a complicated conspiracy theory about Jesus supposedly fathering a child through Mary Magdalene. After Jesus' crucifixion, the mother and child fled to what is today France.

The bloodline of the child was then intermingled with the locals though marriage. These descendants eventually founded the Merovingian Dynasty of Frankish Monarchs. This means that these kings were actual physical descendants of Jesus.

Though this dynasty was deposed in the 8th century, the bloodline which goes back to Jesus still continues to this day. According to Holy Blood, Holy Grail, they may be awaiting the moment to reveal this truth to the world and restore the ancient Holy Roman Empire! Such was the conclusion of the authors of this fictional work.

THE DAVINCI CODE

"The DaVinci Code" has similarities with "Holy Blood, Holy Grail." In each of these books there is no lack of secret societies, cover-ups and conspiracies. In the DaVinci Code, the code to unlock these secrets is supposedly found in Leonardo's most famous paintings. Hence we have the name the "DaVinci code." According to this fictional account, Leonardo was supposedly a member of a secret society which guarded the real truth about Jesus. This society included such notables as Victor Hugo and Sir Isaac Newton.

Although the DaVinci Code acknowledges itself to be a work of fiction, it claims to be accurate in all the historical details it presents. Indeed, it claims to have unraveled the greatest conspiracy in the last 2,000 years. However, the book contains a number of factual errors which unfortunately, the biblically illiterate public does not recognize.

THE FICTIONAL STORY

Like the fictional account in Holy Blood, Holy Grail, in the DaVinci Code Jesus supposedly was married to Mary Magdalene and fathered children through her. This truth about Jesus and Mary has always been known by the leaders of the church. Supposedly, they have helped perpetuate the fraud that Jesus is God the Son. Indeed, according to this fictional account, Jesus was not declared to be God until the council of Nicea in A.D. 325.

To make this story of the divine Jesus acceptable, the church tried to destroy the true gospel accounts of Jesus and substituted false ones in their place. These false gospels, Matthew, Mark, Luke and John, portray Jesus as the divine Son of God rather than the human teacher He really is.

Recently, some of these "true" gospels have been unearthed. These scrolls, which Constantine attempted to destroy, managed to come to light in 1945 at Nag Hammadi, Egypt. They allegedly show the glaring discrepancy between the true story of Jesus and the false one which we find in the four gospels. The fraud of the church is now supposedly there for all to see.

These secret Gnostic Gospels purportedly give us the true account of Jesus. This is the story of the DaVinci Code. Such a message, which denies the fact that Jesus is the one way to reach the one God, has struck a responsive chord in the lives of millions who want to find a way to reject God's truth. Now supposedly they have an historical basis for their unbelief.

WHAT IS THE TRUTH?

Such are the claims of these fictional works. But what is the truth? We can make the following points.

THE TRUTH ABOUT MARY MAGDALENE

The truth of the matter is that Mary Magdalene was a disciple of Jesus. The Bible teaches that she was there at the tomb on Easter Sunday when Jesus came back from the dead.

However, there is no evidence whatsoever that she was married to Jesus, or that there was any romantic involvement between them. Indeed, there is no evidence that Jesus was married to anyone.

At the time of Christ, it was not necessary for godly Jewish males to be married. So this alleged connection between Jesus and Mary Magdalene is mythical. This is one major problem with these conspiracy theories.

THE TRUTH ABOUT THE GOSPELS

Second, the idea that the four gospels were only made authoritative by the church in the fourth century is laughable. Such claims reveal no understanding whatsoever of the historical situation.

For one thing, the New Testament documents were all written by either eyewitnesses or those who recorded eyewitness testimony. The four gospels were received immediately by the followers of Jesus. They were not chosen out of some eighty gospels which were circulating at the time.

By the middle of the second century the four gospels were circulating as a unit. There was never any doubt about their authoritative status—neither were there any rivals.

The Nag Hammadi finds are not accurate accounts of the life of Jesus but rather are the writings of the Gnostics. Gnostics were a secretive sect which held a number of heretical or false beliefs. Their teachings were rejected by the church long before the time of Constantine.

There are further problems. The claim of the DaVinci Code is that Constantine embellished the four gospels to make Jesus godlike. Yet this is not supported by the facts. Indeed, not only were the four gospels written during the lifetime of Jesus' immediate disciples, we today possess manuscript copies of about two thirds of the entire New Testament—copies which were made before the time of Constantine! The text reads the same in the manuscripts which were copied both before and after the time of Constantine. In other words, no embellishments were made.

What the success of these books does demonstrate is the desire of people to escape responsibility before God. If Jesus is not the One whom the four gospels make Him out to be, then we have no accountability to God for how we view Jesus.

If, however, He is the One whom the New Testament says that He is, then everyone, including the authors of these two fictional books, are going to stand before Him someday to be judged.

SUMMARY TO QUESTION 25
COULD THE CHURCH HAVE CONSPIRED TO HIDE THE REAL MESSAGE OF JESUS? (HOLY BLOOD, HOLY GRAIL, THE DAVINCI CODE)

When people do not want to accept the clear teaching of the New Testament with respect to Jesus Christ, they come up with alternative explanations. One such popular view is a conspiracy theory.

Conspiracy theories such as found in such books as "Holy Blood, Holy Grail" and "The DaVinci Code" are popular with many. Indeed, these theories supposedly provide evidence that the New Testament account of Jesus' life and ministry is not what actually occurred.

According to these theories, Jesus fathered a child, or perhaps children, through Mary Magdalene. In addition, Jesus is not the divine Son of God but rather merely a human teacher. Supposedly the church has known this all along but has covered it up in an effort to exercise control over the people. The upshot is that Christianity is not a God-given faith but rather a human-made effort to deify a man who was a simple teacher.

According to the DaVinci Code, the real story of Jesus is found in the Nag Hammadi gospels rather than the four gospels. The true story has now been found!

Obviously, if what these writings are saying is true, then the Christian faith is not what it claims to be. The historical belief of the church is that Jesus Christ is God the Son, the Second Person of the Holy Trinity. He came to earth to reveal to us what God is really like.

When one objectively looks at the evidence, then it becomes clear that the traditional belief of Christians fits the facts—while these other accounts are fictional. A number of points can be made.

First, the four gospels were immediately accepted by the New Testament believers while these other works were soundly rejected. Those who were in a position to know which works were authoritative sources of the life and ministry of Jesus received the four gospels as authentic. On the other hand, they rejected all of these other works. There is no evidence anywhere of some cover up.

In these authoritative works we find that Jesus Christ is revealed as God the Son who became a human being. The gospel writers did not deify Him. Indeed, He has been, and is, the eternal God!

Furthermore, in the four gospels, there is no indication whatsoever that Jesus had any children with Mary Magdalene—or for that matter had any romantic relationship with her at all. This is another myth perpetuated without any evidence.

What all this means is that the God of the Bible does exist and thus humans are answerable to Him.

Therefore, each of us must make a decision for or against Jesus Christ—for He is the One who will determine our eternal destiny.

QUESTION 26

What About The Claims That Jesus Never Said Most Of The Things Attributed To Him In The New Testament? (The Jesus Seminar)

It has been argued that Jesus did not actually do the things the New Testament says that He did, neither did He say the things the New Testament attributes to Him. Therefore, it is not a trustworthy account of the words and deeds of Jesus.

In recent years, this has become a popular notion due to the influence of an organization known as the "Jesus Seminar." Because this group has gathered an enormous amount of publicity from the secular word, and since the issues they bring up have been a traditional source of attack on the reliability of the gospels, we will answer their particular claims. In doing so, we will be laying down principles which will be helpful in answering other objections to the trustworthiness of the gospels.

WHAT IS THE JESUS SEMINAR?

The Jesus Seminar consists of a relatively small group of very liberal New Testament scholars which have been meeting from time to time since 1985. The initial idea was to determine which sayings of Jesus, as recorded in the four gospels, were actually made by Him and which sayings were added later by His disciples, or members of the early church. To make this determination, each saying was voted on by these liberal scholars.

At the outset it must be noted that very few participants in the Jesus Seminar are well-known New Testament scholars. Most of the people who have participated are relatively unknown or totally unknown in the world of New Testament scholarship.

In addition, the entire group consists of mainly American scholars. There has been no real representation from scholarship outside of the United States.

Furthermore, all of them approach this issue with a bias against the supernatural. In other words, they reject all forms of the miraculous.

VOTING WITH BEADS

To discover what these individuals thought Jesus did say, or did not say, each individual saying of Jesus was evaluated and voted upon by casting a bead. When a member voted red, it meant that Jesus must have said this or at least something close to it.

A pink vote meant Jesus probably or may have said something like this. However, a gray vote meant that Jesus did not Himself make the statement but the ideas would have been similar to what He would have held.

Finally, a black bead meant Jesus never said the statement attributed to Him—rather it represents a later tradition in the church.

Not surprisingly, the Jesus Seminar sees very few of the words attributed to Jesus as actually His. Indeed, it is less than 20%.

THIS IS NOT UNIQUE: THE JEFFERSONIAN BIBLE

The idea of determining what Jesus did say, or did not say, or whether He could have performed miracles is not something new. Little known to most people, former United States President Thomas Jefferson did something similar!

Rejecting anything supernatural in the gospels, Jefferson took his scissors and cut out about 90% of the contents of Matthew, Mark, Luke, and John! Like those in the Jesus Seminar, Jefferson rejected anything having to do with the supernatural.

Therefore, the Jesus Seminar is really not doing anything new. Questions about which words of Jesus are authentic, and which may have been added by His disciples, have been going on in academic circles since the eighteenth century. What is unique about this group is the publicity they have received.

Instead of these discussions being confined to the classroom, these individuals have made public what certain liberal scholars have been debating for some time. For this reason, some comments need to be made.

ASSUMPTIONS OF THE JESUS SEMINAR

Before anything about Jesus is evaluated, either the statements attributed to Him, or deeds which He supposedly performed, there are a number of points which are assumed to be true, or pre-supposed by the Jesus Seminar.

We can briefly summarize five of the main assumptions of the Jesus Seminar which lead them to their findings.

1. THE SUPERNATURAL DOES NOT EXIST

To begin with, the members of the Jesus Seminar assume the supernatural does not exist. Therefore, any statements which have to do with the supernatural are rejected out of hand. Their perspective is completely naturalistic. This is primary to their thinking.

2. JESUS COULD NOT HAVE WORKED MIRACLES

The gospels record some thirty-five separate miracles which Jesus performed. Add to this, countless others which were not recorded. The

Jesus Seminar rejects all of these accounts. Why? Because miracles are not possible because the supernatural does not exist!

Therefore, every recorded instance of a miracle must have been a later addition by Jesus' admiring followers—or they can be explained away by natural means.

3. JESUS COULD NOT HAVE PREDICTED THE FUTURE

In the four gospels, we find the Lord Jesus making a number of predictions about the future.

For example, He predicted that He would be betrayed by one of His own disciples. Jesus also said that He would be handed over for crucifixion, and that He would die on a cross in Jerusalem. In addition, according to the New Testament, Jesus Christ also predicted He would come back from the dead three days after His death.

Furthermore, Jesus predicted the destruction of the city of Jerusalem as well as the destruction of the temple within one generation. The New Testament records all of these predictions which Jesus made.

According to the New Testament, the predictions about His betrayal death and resurrection were literally fulfilled. Indeed, the fulfillments are recorded in the pages of the four gospels.

History also tells us that the city of Jerusalem and its temple were destroyed within forty years of Jesus' predictions. This illustrates that Jesus was indeed a prophet.

Yet the Jesus Seminar rejects all of these predictions as coming from Jesus. They assume that these words were placed in His mouth by His later followers.

How do they know this? Again, the answer is simple: No one can predict the future because no human being knows what is going to happen! Therefore, the predictions attributed to Jesus did not come from Him.

4. JESUS NEVER MADE THE FANTASTIC CLAIMS ATTRIBUTED TO HIM

In the New Testament we find that Jesus Christ made a number of incredible claims about Himself. For example, this carpenter from Nazareth claimed to be God Himself, the Savior of the human race. He was the promised Christ, or Messiah, who would deliver Israel from their enemies.

Furthermore, Jesus claimed that He was the One who would judge the human race on Judgment Day. Also, forgiveness of sin was His alone to grant.

In addition, Jesus Christ claimed to be the one way, the only way, by which a person could know the one God. The New Testament says that Jesus made these astounding claims about Himself—as well as many other claims.

However, according to the Jesus Seminar, Jesus made none of these claims. Supposedly, they were attributed to Him by His later followers. He could not have made these claims because Jesus never saw Himself as the Messiah, the Son of God, God Himself, or the Savior of humanity.

5. THE GOSPELS WERE WRITTEN LONG AFTER A.D. 70

As far as the composition of the four gospels is concerned, those of the Jesus Seminar assume that each of them had to have been written after the year A.D. 70.

Why? It is because three out of the four gospels predict the destruction of Jerusalem and the temple. Since Jerusalem and the temple were destroyed in A.D. 70 these gospels must have been written some time after their destruction.

With these assumptions in mind, the members of the Jesus Seminar then go about objectively determining the statements Jesus could have made and those which He could not have made!

EVALUATION OF THE CONCLUSIONS OF THE JESUS SEMINAR

There are so many problems with the assumptions and conclusions of the Jesus Seminar that one hardly knows where to start.

Like Thomas Jefferson a few centuries earlier, the Jesus Seminar commits the same sin of rejecting the possibility of the supernatural. Instead, of looking at the evidence, most of the sayings and deeds of Jesus are ruled out before they are even examined!

Of course, most of the events and sayings recorded in the gospels are going to be rejected by this group because they are done in the context of the supernatural. However, this was the whole point of Jesus coming to earth! Indeed, the New Testament stresses that the coming of Christ was for the purpose of revealing God to humanity. John wrote.

> No one has ever seen God. The only one, himself God, who is in closest fellowship with the Father, has made God known (John 1:18 NET).

Therefore, the Jesus Seminar is guilty of committing the logical fallacy of "begging the question." They are assuming what they should be proving. Why, it may be asked, should we assume that the supernatural does not exist, or that Jesus could not have worked miracles? None of us are in a position to deny the possibility of the miraculous or the supernatural.

Once the possibility of the supernatural has been granted, then one must go about looking at all the evidence. When this occurs, we find that there is sufficient evidence to believe the claims of Jesus. He is indeed the one true God who became a human being.

THE GOSPELS WERE WRITTEN AT AN EARLY DATE

In addition, as we have repeatedly stated, there is good evidence for dating three of the four gospels, and likely all four of them, before the year A.D. 70 when Jerusalem and its temple were destroyed. In fact, there is no compelling reason whatsoever to date them later—unless one wishes to rule out the possibility of predictive prophecy.

CONCLUSION: THEY GIVE US A LESSON IN WHAT NOT TO DO

Thus, the Jesus Seminar provides us with a lesson of what not to do when examining historical claims. All claims should be settled by the weight of the evidence. They should not be determined by what any of us think could or could not have happened. Indeed, NONE of us are in a position to make such an assertion!

SUMMARY TO QUESTION 26
WHAT ABOUT THE CLAIMS THAT JESUS NEVER SAID MOST OF THE THINGS ATTRIBUTED TO HIM IN THE NEW TESTAMENT? (THE JESUS SEMINAR)

The Jesus Seminar consists of a small group of very liberal New Testament scholars who have made a name for themselves by telling the world what they think Jesus Christ actually did say—as well as what He did not say. They believe that *they* can give us the final word on the matter. In the end, they reject most of the sayings of Jesus as authentic.

Of course, they are not unique in doing this. The former president of the United States, Thomas Jefferson, cut all of the miracles out of his Bible when he produced the "Jeffersonian Bible." Yet the Jesus Seminar proudly states that their work is a result of "objective Bible scholarship," and as such they give us the real truth about Jesus. Unhappily many people have believed their claims.

Their conclusions are not surprising when we understand their assumptions. Indeed, before they objectively attempt to determine what Jesus said, or did not say, they rule out anything supernatural.

Accordingly, the Jesus Seminar rejects out of hand the idea of miracles, predictive prophecy, or that Jesus could have claimed to have been God Himself!

For example, since three out of the four gospels predict the coming destruction of the city of Jerusalem, as well as its Holy Temple, the Jesus Seminar dates their composition to a time after Jerusalem was destroyed. Indeed, in view of the fact that they assume that Jesus could not have predicted the future, the Jesus Seminar assumes these documents must have been written sometime after these things took place.

Needless to say this is certainly not the way to approach historical questions. Each claim has to be evaluated on its merit. To reject Jesus Christ and the Christian faith out of hand, without giving it a fair hearing, is an unscholarly thing to do.

Moreover, as we have indicated elsewhere, there are excellent reasons for assuming the four gospels were composed at a very early date. It can be argued that all of them, including the Gospel of John, were written before the year A.D. 70—when Jerusalem was destroyed. This of course would demonstrate that Jesus had the ability to predict the future.

There is something else which must be considered. It is problematic to reject the supernatural out of hand because of what is at stake. According to Jesus Christ, the eternal destiny of each individual, including those of the Jesus Seminar, is determined by how they view Him and His claims.

While the members of the Jesus Seminar may now deny that Jesus said these things, there will come a day when these people, like all of the rest of us, will have to personally answer to Him. When that day comes there will be no denying any of the extraordinary claims about Him which the New Testament records.

What About All The Contradictions In The Gospel Accounts? Doesn't This Make Their Writings Unbelievable?

One of the main arguments that is often used against accepting the reliability of the four gospel's account of the life and the ministry of Jesus are the so-called contradictions that are found. Supposedly, the authors disagree with each other to such a degree that it is hopeless to believe what they wrote. To many, this makes their testimony impossible to accept as true. How do we respond to this objection?

A number of key points need to be made about this issue.

1. THE NATURE OF THE GOSPELS NEEDS TO BE UNDERSTOOD

To begin with, it is important that we understand the nature of the gospels, and of ancient historical writing, before we answer this question. Understanding this, should go a long way into helping us appreciate what the gospels are, as well as what they are not.

2. ANCIENT BIOGRAPHIES WERE NOT WRITTEN THE SAME AS MODERN BIOGRAPHIES

In the ancient world, historical biographies were not written in the same way as modern biographies. Not every major event in the life of the person is listed, but rather only those events that fit the purpose of the author. The writers are selective in what they record and what they omit. This is what we find in the gospels.

In fact, John tells us that he was selective concerning what he wrote. We read.

> Jesus performed many other signs in the presence of His disciples that are not written in this book. But these are written so that you may believe Jesus is the Messiah, the Son of God, and by believing you may have life in His name (John 20:30,31 HCSB).

Consequently, we must read the gospels in light of the stated purpose of the authors. This is why we find in the four gospels an inordinate amount of space devoted to the events leading up to the last week of Jesus' life.

For example, over one half of the Gospel of John is written in this manner. Obviously, it was these events that the author believed were the most important.

3. THE EVENTS WERE NOT ALWAYS WRITTEN IN CHRONOLOGICAL ORDER

Ancient writers did not necessarily write the events they recorded in chronological order. The writers felt free to write according to themes at certain times. In other words, they did not always adhere to strict chronology.

Again, this is what we find in the four gospels. Certain events in Jesus' life are placed in different order in the four gospels. However, the order is not always to be understood chronologically. Ancient readers understood this when they read the gospels—and so should we.

4. STORIES WERE BE CONDENSED AND SUMMARIZED

Furthermore, stories which are recorded can be condensed. Often, the writer summarizes the basic elements of what happened rather than recording every word and everything that occurred.

Again, this is what we find in the four gospels. The same story, told by two different writers, is condensed and summarized by each writer. In doing so, we would expect to find the same general outline but differing details. This is exactly what we do find.

5. HISTORY WAS MORE THAN A RECORD OF EVENTS

In the ancient world, history was never written merely to record what happened. There was always some sort of meaning attached to the events. This is not only true of the four gospels, but in all other ancient historical writings.

The fact that the writers were attempting to promote some cause, or to teach valuable lessons, is how the ancients wrote and recorded history.

This does not take away from their truthfulness. Otherwise, we would have to say we could know nothing of the ancient world since all of its authors were trying to promote some cause—along with their recording of the facts. What is needed is a careful evaluation of what they said and to determine if it matches up with known reality.

6. THE FOUR GOSPELS DO NOT CONTRADICT EACH OTHER ON THE ESSENTIALS

When we examine the four gospels, we must do so in light of how all ancient historical documents were written. Once this is done, many of the so-called problems immediately vanish.

To begin with, it must be noted, that the four gospel writers tell the same basic account of Jesus. There is no contradiction when it comes to the essential facts of Jesus' life and ministry. Any differences are on secondary details.

This is exactly the sort of thing we would expect from four independent authors writing about the same events. We would expect them to tell the same basic story but not with the same exact details. The way in which the gospels now stand shows them to be historically credible. Rather than giving a contradictory picture of Jesus, the differences actually show their independence of one another.

THE PROBLEMS CAN BE HARMONIZED

This brings us to our next point. The differences in detail in the secondary matters, which we do find in the four gospels, can be harmonized. What is necessary is an understanding of how these documents were written, the purpose for their writing, and what they really are saying. Each problem must be examined individually.

Once this is done, a reasonable solution to the problem can be found. This, of course, is only true if the investigator is willing to discover the truth and not assume that the events in Jesus' life, as recorded by the four gospels, must be impossible to harmonize.

CHRISTIANITY WOULD NOT HAVE GROWN WITH FALSE TESTIMONY

There is something else that needs to be considered. The early church grew at an incredible rate. There were thousands of new converts soon after Jesus' death. These new believers were converted in the city of Jerusalem—the same place where the events of Jesus' death and resurrection had just occurred.

If the earliest teaching about Jesus had been in any way false, then there were plenty of people who could have contradicted it. The disciples would have been accused of lying about, or exaggerating, what Jesus said and did. The movement, based upon their crucified leader, would have immediately died.

Instead, the authorities attempted to hush up what really happened at Jesus' empty tomb. Indeed, Jesus' disciples were not called liars when they testified to His miraculous deeds.

This fact can be seen in the statement of Simon Peter to a large crowd on the Day of Pentecost. This event happened only fifty days after Jesus died and rose from the dead. He said the following to this hostile crowd that had gathered.

> People of Israel, listen to these words: Jesus from Nazareth was a very special man. God clearly showed this to you by the miracles, wonders, and signs he did through Jesus. You all know this, because it happened right here among you (Acts 2:22 NCV).

Peter's statement makes it clear that *everyone* knew that Jesus had performed miracles. This was no doubt about this. There would have been no possibly way in which Peter could have made this statement unless it was absolutely true and impossible to refute.

In fact, the crowd would have immediately disbanded if they believed Peter was lying about Jesus' miraculous ability. However, they stayed to listen to what he had to say. Why? Because his claim about Jesus' miracles was something they all knew to be true.

Indeed, the question about Jesus' miracles was always about the source of His power. It was not, "Did He do it," but rather "How did He do it?" Peter told the crowd what they already knew to be true—Jesus Christ was a miracle worker. He then went on to explain the greatest miracle of all. Jesus had risen from the dead! His message was received by the crowd and three thousand people were converted that day.

THE BURDEN OF PROOF IS ON THOSE WHO DENY THE TESTIMONY OF THE GOSPELS

With these facts in mind, the burden of proof is on those who would attempt to deny the gospel accounts of Jesus. There must be evidence brought forward to reject the testimony of the four evangelists.

While the gospels will meet any reasonable standard of proof, they will not, however, meet an impossible standard. Unfortunately, this is the standard some people set. By definition, they make it impossible to demonstrate the accuracy of the gospels.

However, unreliability must be proven, not merely assumed. Implausible theories of what might have happened will not do. What is needed are facts. When the facts are honestly considered, the story of Jesus not only holds up, it passes all reasonable tests of what we would expect of any ancient historical writers.

In sum, we conclude that the gospels are trustworthy documents. The supposed contradictions can be harmonized—if one is willing to take the time and consider all of the evidence. Unfortunately, too few people ever do this.

SUMMARY TO QUESTION 27
WHAT ABOUT ALL THE CONTRADICTIONS IN THE GOSPEL ACCOUNTS? DOESN'T THIS MAKE THEIR WRITINGS UNBELIEVABLE?

One of the most often brought up objections to accepting the New Testament account of Jesus is the so-called contradictions in the gospel accounts. Indeed, problems with chronology are mentioned along with stories giving different details, etc. These problems are used to deny the trustworthiness of the story. If the writers could not get their own stories straight, then why should we believe what they say?

However, once we have an understanding of ancient historical writing, many of the problems will immediately go away. We can make the following observations.

For one thing, ancient biographies were not written in the same manner as modern biographies. At Jesus' time, biographies did not necessarily cover all the events in a person's life. Instead the writers were selective in what they wrote. The New Testament writers tell us that selectivity was also their goal. This is why we find the emphasis on certain events in Jesus life—in particular His last week on earth before His death.

In addition, the fact that the events are not always listed chronologically is not a problem. Ancient biographies were not always chronological.

Furthermore, that the gospels sometimes condense and summarize stories about Jesus is likewise not problematic. This was how ancient writing was often done. Again, the original readers would have understood this technique.

We must also remember that we are not simply looking at the listing of historical events in the gospels. While the events were historical, they are more than mere history. Indeed, there is always a divine meaning that goes along with the events. In other words, everything listed has meaning attached to it.

With respect to the so-called contradictions, the main events in Jesus' life, the essentials, are agreed upon by all four gospels. It is only in the secondary details that we find minor differences. Furthermore, these differences can be reasonably harmonized—if one is willing to take the time to examine them.

What also needs to be considered is the rapid growth of Christianity in the ancient world. The fact that Christianity grew as quickly as it did shows that the people readily accepted its message. If the authoritative documents contained hopeless contradictions, it is hard to imagine how the faith spread like it did.

This being the case, we have every reason to believe the four gospels are an accurate description of what Jesus said and did. The burden of proof is on those who deny what they say. To make their case they must present convincing evidence against the trustworthiness of the gospels. This evidence has never been forthcoming from unbelievers—for the simple reason that it does not exist! In sum, the gospels are accurate accounts of Jesus' life and ministry.

QUESTION 28

Did The Gospel Writers Use Previous Written Documents To Compile Their Accounts? (The Synoptic Problem And The Q Source)

One of the most complex problems confronting those who make a study of the four gospels is the determination of the relationship between them. There is much material common to them—but there are also differences.

Many questions arise. What is the order in which the four gospels were written? Were the gospels based upon earlier written sources? Is it possible that one or more of the gospels was originally written in a language other than Greek? Did Matthew and Luke use Mark when they composed their gospel? Was there an earlier written source that is behind some of the material in the gospels? These issues are part of what is called the "synoptic problem."

SOME UNDERSTANDING OF THE ISSUES IS NECESSARY

Our desire here is to provide basic overview of this issue. It is important that each student of Scripture have at least some acquaintance with these questions. However, any detailed explanation is beyond the scope of what we are trying to do.

THE SYNOPTIC PROBLEM EXPLAINED

The synoptic problem can be summarized as follows. The first three gospels, Matthew, Mark, and Luke are called the "synoptic gospels." This comes from two Greek words which mean, "to see together." The word was used to explain how these gospels can be arranged, harmonized section by section, and viewed together.

When the first three gospels are looked at together, a number of things become obvious. The accounts in Matthew, Mark, and Luke have striking resemblances. The wording is exactly the same, or nearly the same, in many passages. However, minor differences also continually appear between these three gospels. How can we account for these resemblances and differences in Matthew, Mark and Luke? This is the synoptic problem.

THERE ARE MANY THEORIES TO EXPLAIN WHAT WE FIND

In gospel studies, there have been a number of theories that have attempted to account for the resemblances, as well as the differences between the first three gospels—the synoptic gospels. We can list them as follows.

OPTION 1: THE GOSPELS ARE TOTALLY INDEPENDENT OF EACH OTHER

This first option sees each gospel as completely independent of the other two. In other words, there is no literary relationship between them whatsoever. The literary resemblances can be attributed to the gospel writers all drawing on the same oral tradition about Jesus. The oral tradition was so fixed at an early date that the gospel writers often would have the same word-for-word description of what Jesus said and did—or at least a description that was very similar. According to this point of view, there was no written source used by any of the gospel writers.

OPTION 2: THE GOSPELS HAVE SOME LITERARY DEPENDENCE

Others believe the resemblances between the first three gospels cannot be accounted for by oral transmission alone. They see some type of literary dependence as necessary because of the way the gospels now stand. This being the case, there are a number of theories of literary dependence which have arisen which try to explain the agreements between the gospels. In doing so, they also try to determine the order in which these works were originally written. The most popular are as follows.

MARK WAS WRITTEN FIRST

The most popular theory in our present day, to explain the similarities and differences among the first three gospels, assumes Mark was the first gospel written and that the other two synoptic gospels writers, Matthew and Luke, made use of Mark when they composed their gospel.

In addition, they also had another written source which basically consisted of Jesus' sayings. This source is usually known as "Q" from the German word quelle meaning "source." Apart from Mark and the Q source, both Matthew and Luke incorporated material in their gospel that was unique to them. For simplicity sake, the material Matthew used is called "M" and the material Luke used is called "L."

MATTHEW WAS WRITTEN FIRST

While the idea that Mark was written first is the most dominant view today, it is not without its detractors. A minority of scholars believe that Matthew was written first, and that Luke used Matthew to compose his gospel. Mark, instead of being the first gospel written, was actually written after Matthew and Luke. This theory holds that Mark's Gospel is a combination of Matthew and Luke. This theory has no need for any "Q" source.

This theory is consistent with the ancient evidence. The unanimous testimony of the early church was that Matthew wrote first. There is also strong evidence that Luke wrote after Matthew and used his gospel is putting together his own account. Mark, which records the preaching of Simon Peter, was written after both Matthew and Luke. It is said that Peter used both of these works to put together his messages which was incorporated by Mark into a written document.

OTHER THEORIES AND OTHER VERSIONS

There are many other theories, which are not as popular as these two, which attempt to explain the relationship between the first three gospels. In addition, even these popular theories are found in many versions. This all adds further complications to this issue.

OBSERVATIONS ON THE SYNOPTIC PROBLEM

The synoptic problem is indeed complicated. We will only make a few simple observations concerning this difficult issue

THERE IS NO CONSENSUS AMONG BIBLE-BELIEVING SCHOLARS ON THIS ISSUE

Today, there are Bible-believers that hold to each of the theories we have listed, as well as other viewpoints which we have not given. We must emphasize that there is no consensus as to which theory is correct. Each has its advocates who make, what they believe, are solid arguments for their position. Every one of these theories has their strengths and weaknesses. Indeed, it seems that none is without its problems.

This being the case, there is no "Christian" position on this issue. Consequently, we need to be careful to assume there is only one particular way in which this matter can be resolved.

Q IS ONLY A HYPOTHESIS

While people speak of a "Q" document as though its existence is certain, we must remember that it is only a hypothetical document. There are credible, if not convincing, theories of the composition of the first three gospels that have no need for any such written work.

Therefore, we must be careful how much we assume about this alleged document that no one has ever seen, no one in the ancient world admitted to its existence, and many find no need of today to account for the gospels in their present form.

There is something else. Unfortunately, some liberal scholars use this hypothetical Q document to argue that the original Jesus was a non-supernatural Jesus. They have supposedly discovered the earliest form of the Q sayings in which Jesus was a mere human teacher, not a miracle worker, or the Son of God. The sad thing is that they have convinced a number of people that this is where the evidence leads us.

Yet, it has been shown by others, that even if Q did exist, which we do not know for certain, it still portrays a supernatural Jesus who performed miracles and made divine claims about Himself. The supernatural Jesus is still with us—with or without Q.

There have indeed been abuses by those who argue for some type of written source behind Matthew and Luke. However, it is not impossible that a list or Jesus' sayings did circulate in some written form at an early date. We cannot, and we should not, rule out this possibility ahead of time. What we should rule out, is the way in which some scholars take this hypothetical document, put together a hypothetical history of it, and then deny everything sacred that the New Testament teaches about Jesus. This is neither a rational nor a scholarly thing to do.

However, having said that, it must be pointed out that the early church unanimously taught that Matthew was the first gospel written. This evidence should not be ignored because these people would be in a position to know the order in which the gospels were composed. With this continuous testimony that we have from these church leaders, it seems like Q is unnecessary. While the idea that Matthew was written first is still in the minority among present-day New Testament, specialists, it seems for a number of reasons to be the best way to understand the totality of the evidence.

THE GOSPELS, AS THEY NOW STAND, ARE GOD'S HOLY WORD

Whatever the eventual solution may be concerning the synoptic problem, the important thing is for us to understand that the end result is God's divinely inspired, inerrant Word to the human race. The important thing is to read and study the gospels as we now have them.

While there is a place for trying to solve the synoptic problem, we should not spend all of our time and effort trying to determine how they came to be in their present form. God has given these works to us so that we can study and learn from them as they are now written. This is where we should place our energies.

SUMMARY TO QUESTION 28
DID THE GOSPEL WRITERS USE PREVIOUS WRITTEN SOURCES TO COMPILE THEIR ACCOUNTS? (THE SYNOPTIC PROBLEM AND THE Q SOURCE)

One of the continuing issues in the study of the gospels is the relationship between the first three gospels. Which one was written first? Matthew, Mark and Luke have much in common but there are also many differences between them. A number of theories attempt to account for the gospels as we now find them.

Some believe the differences, as well as the agreements, can be accounted for by factors which do not assume that there were previously written documents. Common oral tradition is cited to account for the word-for-word agreements. It is argued that many of Jesus' words and deeds were put into a fixed form early in the history of the church. This is why we find word-for-word agreement in many cases.

Others, however, believe the agreements are too precise without assuming some sort of literary dependence. The most popular theory is that Mark was written first and that Matthew and Luke used Mark in composition of their gospels. Material found in both Matthew and Luke, but not found in Mark, is supposedly from a written source called Q. The material unique to Matthew is called "M" while the material unique to Luke is termed "L." As one can readily observe, all of this can get rather confusing!

However, many others think, as the early church unanimously believed, that Matthew was the first gospel written. Luke came next in order and then Mark. This takes away any need for a Q source. Bible believing scholars have different perspectives on this issue. However, there is no real reason to doubt the ancient testimony and thus assume Matthew was the first gospel written.

The key is to study the gospels as they now stand instead of attempting to determine which one was written first, and who may, or may not, have copied whom. Indeed, the all-knowing and all-powerful God of the Bible has allowed these four documents to come down to us in the fixed form that we now find them. This is how He wants us to study them—as we now find them. This is what we should be doing.

Did The Early Church Invent Some, If Not All, Of The Sayings Of Jesus?

One of the claims which is often made against the authenticity of the gospels is that the New Testament church, rather than accurately recording what Jesus said and did, read their own words and current needs back into four gospels.

When an issue arose in the early years of the church, and an authoritative answer was needed to deal with the problem, the believers merely created an incident where Jesus dealt with the matter. They would make Him comment on the issue so that they had authoritative answers to their current needs. Consequently, they would create an historical situation, and then have Jesus address the problem in His day. This is why we find the gospels in their present form.

THE NEW TESTAMENT PROPHETS SPOKE FOR THE LORD

In support of this view is the existence of the New Testament prophets. These prophets would preface their authoritative words to other believers by phrases such as, "thus says the Lord." Since their words were seen to be the "words of the Lord," there was no distinction made between what they said and what Jesus said.

Thus, the words that we find in the four gospels, which are attributed to Jesus, are not really what He said at all. Rather it was what the church put into His mouth to meet their needs of the time. This view, of course, would rob the gospels of any authority—as well as having the church creating Jesus rather than Jesus creating the church. What are we to make of such an accusation?

RESPONSE

A number of responses can be made to the idea that the church created the words of Jesus. They can be listed as follows.

1. JESUS CREATED THE CHURCH, IT DID NOT CREATE HIM

To begin with, Jesus Christ created the church—it certainly did not create Him. Jesus made this clear in His famous statement to Simon Peter. He said.

> Now I say to you that you are Peter, and upon this rock I will build my church, and all the powers of hell will not conquer it (Matthew 16:18 NLT).

Jesus said that He will build *His* church. In doing so, He is in complete control of all things. Otherwise, the figure of Jesus Christ is reduced to the creative abilities of His disciples. However, any superficial reading of the four gospels will quickly demonstrate that these men were not religious geniuses! They certainly did not have the ability to create Jesus. The New Testament church is the creation of Jesus.

2. JESUS' WORDS WERE DISTINGUISHED FROM THOSE OF OTHERS

There is something else we must appreciate. The New Testament church purposefully and carefully made the distinction between what Jesus actually said during His public ministry, with the events that occurred afterward.

For example, the Apostle Paul distinguished between his words and the words of Jesus. He noted these differences in his first letter to the Corinthians when he wrote the following.

> To the rest I say—I, not the Lord—if a brother has a wife who is not a believer and she is happy to live with him, he should not divorce her (1 Corinthians 7:12 NET).

Paul was clear to distinguish between what he actually said, and what Jesus said. There was no confusing of the two.

3. THE WORDS OF THE PROPHETS WERE TO BE TESTED

Those who spoke in place of the Lord were called prophets. They did speak for the Lord. However, believers were to test the prophets. Paul wrote to the Corinthians about this necessity.

> Two or three prophets should speak and let others evaluate what is said (1 Corinthians 14:29 NET).

The people were told to evaluate the words of the prophets.

Paul said the same thing to the Thessalonians regarding prophetic messages. Indeed, he command them to test everything. He wrote.

> Do not treat prophecies with contempt. But examine all things; hold fast to what is good (1 Thessalonians 5:20,21 NET).

The words of the prophets were to be tested, not blindly trusted.

In addition, the phrase the "Word of the Lord" coming from the prophets, does not necessarily mean the direct Word of Jesus. The Lord is God's name. It can refer to Jesus, or it can refer to God the Father, or to God the Holy Spirit. Often it is just a general term for God Himself. It depends upon the context.

There is no evidence whatsoever that when the prophets of the early church were saying, "Thus says the Lord" they were claiming that these words were spoken by Jesus during His public ministry.

THEY WERE NEVER TOLD TO TEST JESUS' WORDS

While the words of the prophets were to be tested and evaluated, never do we find Jesus' authentic words being put to the test. They were not to test Jesus' words—they were to believe and obey them! This is the distinction which is always made by the Lord Jesus and the New Testament prophets. Their words were to be tested—Jesus' words were to be believed.

In addition, we should note that the words of Jesus are always placed in an historical context in the four gospels. The gospels record that Jesus spoke certain words on specific occasions to specific people. They do not merely consist of a list of Jesus' sayings that were given without any historical situation.

MANY ISSUES THE CHURCH FACED WERE NOT COVERED BY JESUS' WORDS

There is something else. Many issues, that became important in the early years of the church, were not covered in the gospels, or dealt with by Jesus. Questions such as the role of women, how the Jews and Gentiles were to function together as believers in Jesus, the existence and exercise of spiritual gifts, as well as a number of other problems facing the church, were not addressed by Jesus, or recorded in the four gospels.

If the church was merely attempting to answer these questions by appealing to Jesus, then they would have had created instances where He spoke authoritatively on these matters.

Yet, the four gospels are silent on these, as well as a number of other issues that were controversial in the early church. It was only as the church grew that these issues became prominent. When they needed answering, these issues were not read back into the gospels to have Jesus supply the answer—rather they were answered by the leaders of the church, the apostles of Jesus.

AN ILLUSTRATION OF WHY THE CHURCH DID NOT CREATE JESUS' WORDS: THE TEMPLE TAX

We can provide one clear illustration of why the gospels do not reflect problems that arose later in the church. This concerns the payment or non-payment of the temple tax. Matthew records what occurred.

> After they arrived in Capernaum, the collectors of the temple tax came to Peter and said, "Your teacher pays the double drachma tax, doesn't he?" (Matthew 17:24 NET).

Jesus, we are told, did indeed pay the tax. This temple tax was an annual tax that Jewish males paid to support the temple in Jerusalem. While this was not a controversial issue in His day, it soon became one after Jerusalem, and the temple, were destroyed. After A.D. 70, the temple tax was still to be paid by the Jews, yet it was diverted to pay for the upkeep of the temple of the god Jupiter in Rome. Though the Jewish temple no longer stood, the Romans insisted the Jews were to continue to pay the temple tax. The idea that Jesus would encourage payment to this temple dedicated to a pagan god is preposterous.

Yet, if we are to assume that the early church merely read their problems back into the gospel accounts, this is exactly what we would have to conclude—for Jesus encouraged payment of the temple tax. The fact that Jesus paid the temple tax is one of many evidences that the gospels contain the exact words and teaching of Jesus from His time. Indeed, they are not from a later period in the history of the church.

We conclude that the church was careful to distinguish what Jesus said and did during His earthly ministry and the issues that needed authoritative answers in the later years. There is no evidence whatsoever that they conveniently had Jesus answer these questions during His public ministry by putting words into His mouth.

SUMMARY TO QUESTION 29
DID THE EARLY CHURCH INVENT SOME, IF NOT ALL, OF THE SAYINGS OF JESUS?

One of objections that is often brought up against trusting what is found in the Matthew, Mark, Luke and John concerns Jesus' words as found in the gospels, and the New Testament church actually inventing them. It has been alleged that much of what is attributed to Jesus in the four gospels was, in point of fact, put into His mouth by the early church.

Supposedly when certain problems arose, and a solution was needed, the early church created a situation in which Jesus answered the problem.

Though such a thing never happened in Jesus' life and ministry, the New Testament "prophets" used this technique to teach God's truth to the people. Therefore, much of what we read about Jesus in the four gospels consists of situations which never took place.

This theory, while popular in some circles, is without any foundation whatsoever. The evidence shows no such thing. Jesus' words were always distinguished from the words of the early Christians. Indeed, they were never mingled. For example, Paul the apostle made it clear when he was speaking and when the Lord spoke. He never combined his words with those of Jesus.

Furthermore, we find that the words of New Testament prophets were to be weighed and evaluated. They were not blindly accepted by the early believers. On the other hand, Jesus' words were never to be evaluated. They were to be believed and obeyed.

In addition, the issue of paying the temple tax shows that the early church was not putting later issues into the mouth of Jesus. The temple tax which Jesus paid for upkeep of the temple in Jerusalem was later used by the Romans to pay for the upkeep of the temple of Jupiter in Rome.

This occurred after the temple in Jerusalem was destroyed. There was fierce opposition among Jews and Christians about paying this tax. There is no reason whatsoever to believe the church created a situation where Jesus would encourage payment of this tax for the upkeep of a pagan building.

This illustrates that there was no putting words in Jesus' mouth by the early church leaders to settle contemporary issues. The gospels contain the things Jesus actually said and did. We have no reason to believe that they were invented by His earliest followers.

QUESTION 30

Are The Four Gospels
Historically Accurate?

The four gospels have many references to people, places, customs, and events as they record the life and ministry of Jesus. The evidence from the New Testament is that the writers of the four gospels have desired to give us a truthful historical portrait of Jesus and His ministry. The four gospels writers were also in a position to do this.

This being the case, questions naturally arise: "Have they given us a picture of Jesus that matches us with known reality? Did the people actually exist? Are the places real places? Did the events really occur?"

THE EVIDENCE SHOWS THEY ARE TRUSTWORTHY

While it is not possible to independently verify everything that the four gospels record, it is possible to see if what they record matches up with what we know about first-century life in that part of the world.

When we do this, we find that what they have written does indeed match up with the known history of that period. The following points need to be made about this very important issue.

1. THE PEOPLE ACTUALLY EXISTED

The people that the four gospels mention were historical figures. There is no doubt about this. For example, Pontius Pilate, Herod the Great,

Herod Antipas, and Tiberius Caesar are known to have truly existed. Consequently, we are dealing with real people who really lived at that time and place in history.

2. PONTIUS PILATE WAS PREFECT OF JUDEA

For many years there were questions about the existence and the actual title of Pontius Pilate—the Roman governor who presided over the trial of Jesus. In later Roman writers, as well as almost all Bible reference works, Pilate is referred to as the "procurator" of Judea. According to the New Testament, he is called a "governor" rather than a procurator.

In 1961, on the coast of Israel in the town of Caesarea, the discovery was made of a two by three-foot stone that had a Latin inscription written upon it. The translation of the inscription reads as follows:

> Pontius Pilate, Prefect of Judea, has presented the Tiberieum
> to the Caesareans

This is the first archaeological evidence for the existence of Pontius Pilate. What is interesting about the inscription is the title that he is given—"Prefect of Judea." We now know that the title "procurator" was not used at the time for the Roman governors. This title only came into usage at a later time.

In fact, it was during the reign of the emperor Claudius, A.D. 41-54, that the title of the Roman governors shifted from prefect to procurator. Although many of the later Roman writers gave Pilate the incorrect title, the New Testament did not. It calls him a governor, not a procurator. Thus, in its description of Pilate the New Testament is accurate.

THE TWO HERODS WERE HISTORICAL CHARACTERS

The gospels mention two people by the name of Herod. We have the listing of Herod the Great as well as Herod the Tetrarch.

HEROD THE GREAT

Herod the Great was the ruler of Judea at the time of the birth of Christ. In fact, he is mentioned in connection with the Lord's birth. We read of this in Matthew.

> Jesus was born in the town of Bethlehem in Judea, during the reign of King Herod. About that time some wise men from eastern lands arrived in Jerusalem, asking, "Where is the newborn king of the Jews? We have seen his star as it arose, and we have come to worship him" (Matthew 2:1,2 NLT).

From a number of sources, we know that Herod the Great existed. First century writer Flavius Josephus tells us much of Herod's history.

Also coins have been discovered that have the inscription "Herod the King." At the site of Masada, where hundreds of Jews went to their deaths in defiance of the Roman army, a potsherd has been found that says "Herod, King of the Jews." Consequently, his existence is unquestionably confirmed.

HEROD THE TETRARCH

During Jesus' public ministry, some thirty years later, another Herod is mentioned. He is known as "Herod the tetrarch." We also read of him in Matthew. It says.

> At that time Herod the tetrarch heard the reports about Jesus (Matthew 14:1 NIV).

Once more, we are dealing with genuine history. We know that Herod the Tetrarch existed because of the writings of first century Jewish historian Flavius Josephus as well as coins that were minted that have inscribed the words, "Herod the tetrarch." The gospels are once again found to be accurate.

THE BURIAL BOX OF THE HIGH PRIEST CAIAPHAS HAS LIKELY BEEN FOUND

A stunning example of extra-biblical confirmation of the existence of a New Testament character is found in the discovery of the bones of the High Priest Caiaphas. The New Testament says that Caiaphas is the one who presided over one of the trials of Jesus. Matthew writes about him and gives the following description.

> And those who had laid hold of Jesus led Him away to Caiaphas the high priest, where the scribes and the elders were assembled (Matthew 26:57 NKJV).

In 1990, the bones of Caiaphas were discovered in a limestone ossuary, or burial box that was found in the old city of Jerusalem. The inscription on the ornate burial box read, "Joseph, son of Caiaphas." This was the first physical remains that have been discovered of a person mentioned in Scripture.

These are a few of the many examples that could be given of extra biblical confirmation of New Testament characters. The point is simple. The people whom the gospels mentioned were real people. They were not mythical characters.

THE CITIES EXISTED WHERE THE GOSPELS SAY THEY DID

The gospels also record various places where the ministry of Jesus took place. We find that the cities that are mentioned in the four gospels are known to have existed in the first century. The exact location of almost all of them has been firmly established. This includes such cities as Nazareth, Cana, Bethlehem, Capernaum, Chorazin, Bethsaida, and Tiberius. In other words, we are dealing with real places that existed during a definite time in history.

THE HOUSES AND STRUCTURES MENTIONED ACTUALLY EXISTED

There were certain physical structures that are mentioned in the gospels that are now known to exist. For example, we have a number of references to synagogues where Jesus taught.

However, for a long time there were no physical remains of any first century synagogue that had been discovered. This led critics to deny that Jesus actually taught in synagogues. Yet this is no longer the case. A number of first century synagogues have now been discovered.

In the city of Capernaum, ruins have been found that may have been the actual house of Simon Peter. A fifth century church was built over the remains of a first century house. If these are the ruins of Simon Peter's house, then this is the place where Jesus stayed while in the city of Capernaum.

THE WRITERS KNEW THE LOCAL CUSTOMS OF THE TIMES

The customs that were practiced in the first-century are consistent with that which is recorded in the four gospels. In fact, we find that these customs are related in a way that is minutely accurate. For example, in the Gospel of Luke we read the following account.

> Soon afterward Jesus went to a town called Nain, and his disciples and a large crowd went with him. As he approached the town gate, a man who had died was being carried out, the only son of his mother (who was a widow), and a large crowd from the town was with her. When the Lord saw her, he had compassion for her and said to her, "Do not weep." Then he came up and touched the bier, and those who carried it stood still. He said, "Young man, I say to you, get up!" So the dead man sat up and began to speak, and Jesus gave him back to his mother (Luke 7:11-15 NET).

At the time of Christ, there were different customs with respect to women walking in a funeral procession. In Judea, the area around Jerusalem, the custom was for the women to walk behind the funeral procession.

However, in the Galilee region, the custom was reversed. The women walked in front of the funeral procession. The description given by

Luke demonstrates the minute accuracy of his account. Jesus began to talk to the mother of the dead child, and then touched the coffin of the dead man. At that time the funeral procession stopped—because it was following behind her and the coffin.

This would have only been true in the Galilee region. If this story would have been placed in Judea, then it would not have happened this way— the women would have followed the procession. The fact that Luke incidentally notes that the procession stopped when Jesus touched the coffin shows the minute accuracy of his account. Many other examples could be given.

THE EVENTS ACTUALLY OCCURRED AS THE GOSPELS SAY THEY DID

There is non-biblical confirmation for some of the events recorded in the four gospels. We can give the following example.

Luke tells us of a census that was to be taken for the Roman world. He explains what occurred in this manner.

> Now in those days a decree went out from Caesar Augustus to register all the empire for taxes. This was the first registra-tion, taken when Quirinius was governor of Syria. Everyone went to his own town to be registered (Luke 2:1-3 NET).

From secular sources we know that this type of census did occur on a regular basis in the Roman Empire. While there is an issue with respect to the timing of the census to which Luke gives reference, there is no doubt that such a census took place. Again, we have further evidence of the accuracy of the gospels.

CONCLUSION: THE GOSPELS FIT THE HISTORICAL EVIDENCE

Therefore, when all the evidence is considered, we find that the gospels match up with the known history of that time. The people were real people, the cities actually existed where the New Testament says they did, the customs were exactly as stated, and the events, like the enrollment of the people recorded by Luke, in fact, occurred.

The fact of their historical accuracy has important implications for us. If the writers were correct in the references we can check out, then they should be given the benefit of the doubt in matters we cannot check out. This is a reasonable way in which to deal with this issue of historical reliability.

Scholar Craig Evans offers a fitting summary of the matter.

> There is also a very important argument in favor of the general reliability of the New Testament Gospels, and that concerns what is called verisimilitude; that is, what the gospels describe matches the way things really were in the early first-century Jewish Palestine. The New Testament gospels and Acts exhibit a great deal of verisimilitude. They speak of real people (such as Pontius Pilate, Herod Antipas, Annas, Caiaphas, Herod Agrippa I and II, Felix and Festus) and real events (deaths of John the Baptist and Agrippa I). They speak of real places (villages, cities, roads, lakes and mountains) that are clarified and corroborated by other historical sources and by archaeology. They speak of real customs (Passover, purity, Sabbath, divorce law), institutions (synagogue, temple), offices/officers (priests, tax collectors Roman governors, Roman centurions) and beliefs (of Pharisees and Sadducees; interpretation of Scripture). Jesus' engagement with his contemporaries, both supporters and opponents, reflects an understanding of Scripture and theology that we now know, thanks to the Dead Sea Scrolls and related literature, to have been current in pre-70 Jewish Palestine (Craig Evans, *Jesus and His World: The Archaeological Evidence*, Westminster, John Knox Press, Louisville, Kentucky, 2012, p. 9)

While it ultimately comes down to faith, it is certainly reasonable and sensible faith that is exercised toward believing in the historical accuracy of the gospels. Indeed, it is not blind faith!

SUMMARY TO QUESTION 30
ARE THE FOUR GOSPELS HISTORICALLY ACCURATE?

Jesus Christ came to this world at a certain time in history. His three-year public ministry is recorded in four written works known as "gospels." In these gospels there are a number or references to people, places, customs, and events. Since Christianity is a religion that claims certain events took place in history, these historical references must be accurate. As we look at the evidence we will discover that the gospel writers were indeed historically correct in their references.

The four gospels give an accurate portrayal of people, places, customs, and events in the land of Israel in the first century. For one thing, we know that the people mentioned are historical characters—they actually did exist. Indeed, secular history records the existence of such people as the Caesar's, Herod the Great, Herod the Tetrarch, Caiaphas the High Priest, and Pontius Pilate. Therefore, the characters in the gospel accounts were actual people who lived at a certain time in history. There is no doubt about this.

In addition, the places mentioned by Matthew, Mark, Luke and John match up geographically with what we know about first century Israel. Most of the cities where Jesus' ministry and miracles took place have now been identified with certainty. In other words, there were such cities as Bethsaida, Capernaum, Nazareth, and Bethlehem and we now know their precise geographical location.

The customs also fit well with the times. In fact, the recording of certain customs by the gospel writers demonstrates their minute accuracy. This indicates that they had to have been present to know these specific customs and laws at the time. Indeed, only those living at that era would have known these unique customs of the times.

Events recorded in the four gospels are also consistent with what we know occurred at that particular time in history. From secular history we know that a census, or enrollment, was taken of the people. Thus, the story of Joseph and Mary coming to Bethlehem to enroll in the census makes historical sense.

In addition to all of this, there is nothing found in the four gospels which would not fit with that time and place in history. Everything recorded is consistent with what we know of the times. This is important to note. We do not find anything that would not fit that historical period. This gives further indication that we have firsthand testimony of the things which took place. In other words, we have eyewitness testimony.

Consequently, the historical testimony of the writers of the four gospels should be taken seriously. Realizing this gives us confidence in everything else they wrote. Indeed, if they were accurate in their historical references, then they should be given the benefit of the doubt in the other things which they recorded about Jesus. This includes His words as well as His miraculous deeds.

In sum, there is every reason to believe that the gospels are what the church has always believed them to be—the reliable, historically accurate Word of God.

Did Jesus
Write Anything?

The New Testament gives the account of the life of Jesus Christ written by His disciples. The question is often asked about Jesus is, "Why don't we have anything in writing from Him?" Would He have been able to write? If so, then why didn't He leave us with any written record?

These are fair questions. We can make the following observations in response to them.

1. JESUS COULD READ AND WRITE

The New Testament informs us that Jesus could both read and write. The Gospel of Luke tells us of an incident where Jesus read from the prophet Isaiah. It reads as follows.

And he came to Nazareth, where he had been brought up. And as was his custom, he went to the synagogue on the Sabbath day, and he stood up to read. And the scroll of the prophet Isaiah was given to him. He unrolled the scroll and found the place where it was written, "The Spirit of the Lord is upon me, because he has anointed me

> to proclaim good news to the poor. He has sent me to pro-
> claim liberty to the captives and recovering of sight to the
> blind, to set at liberty those who are oppressed, to proclaim
> the year of the Lord's favor." And he rolled up the scroll and

gave it back to the attendant and sat down. And the eyes of all in the synagogue were fixed on him. And he began to say to them, "Today this Scripture has been fulfilled in your hearing" (Luke 4:16-21 ESV).

From this passage we can see that Jesus certainly had the ability to read. Indeed, Christ found the place in the scroll where He wanted to read, and then He read the desired portion. Furthermore, He stopped reading at the appropriate time. Thus, His ability to read a text is beyond all doubt. Jesus could read.

2. JESUS WROTE SOMETHING ON THE GROUND

There is a passage found in John's Gospel that demonstrates Jesus also had the ability to write. It reads as follows.

> As he was speaking, the teachers of religious law and Pharisees brought a woman they had caught in the act of adultery. They put her in front of the crowd. "Teacher," they said to Jesus, "this woman was caught in the very act of adultery. The law of Moses says to stone her. What do you say?" They were trying to trap him into saying something they could use against him, but Jesus stooped down and wrote in the dust with his finger. They kept demanding an answer, so he stood up again and said, "All right, stone her. But let those who have never sinned throw the first stones!'" Then he stooped down again and wrote in the dust. When the accusers heard this, they slipped away one by one, beginning with the oldest, until only Jesus was left in the middle of the crowd with the woman (John 8:3-9 NLT).

The fact that Jesus could write is taught in this passage. We should not assume that He just doodled on the ground. He wrote something that caused the religious leaders to leave the scene. Exactly what He wrote has been the subject of endless speculation. However, no one knows for certain what He wrote.

Although the authenticity of this passage is in dispute, since it does not exist in some early manuscripts of Johns' gospel, almost everyone agrees that it reflects an actual occurrence in the ministry of Jesus. Therefore, from the evidence we can conclude that Jesus could both read and write.

3. WHY DIDN'T HE WRITE SOMETHING FOR US?

If Jesus could read and write, then why didn't He leave behind anything written for humanity? The answer is we simply do not know why Jesus did not write any texts setting down His teachings—or give us any firsthand knowledge of His innermost thoughts.

These questions, which have been a puzzle to people since the first century, have no real answer.

DO WE HAVE A LETTER FROM JESUS?

There is an ancient letter that purports to have been written from Jesus. It is known as, "The Letter to King Abgar." Abgar was a real king who reigned from A.D. 9 to A.D. 46 in what is in modern-day Turkey. As the story goes, King Abgar wrote first to Jesus requesting a miracle. He supposedly wrote.

> And when I heard all those things about you, I considered that you are either God himself who has come down from heaven to act like this, or that you are the Son of God doing such things. Therefore I am writing to you and ask you to visit me and cure my illness. Incidentally, I have heard that the Jews are grumbling about you and wish you harm. I have a city, rather small, but noble, and it is sufficient for us both.

Abgar wanted a visit from Jesus. He had heard about Jesus' healing ability as well as the unwanted attention that He was receiving from the religious rulers. Abgar offered his protection.

THE REPLY OF JESUS TO KING ABGAR

It is recorded that Jesus replied by means of a courier. He began the letter with a blessing that is also found in John's gospel.

Blessed are you, who has believed in me without having seen me.

Jesus, according to His letter, declined Abgar's invitation because He had not fulfilled His public ministry. However, Jesus wrote that He would send one of His disciples after His ascension, "so that he may cure your illness and give life to you and to those who are with you." According to this letter, Jesus would honor Abgar's request for help.

THERE WAS A HAPPY ENDING TO THE STORY

According to the fourth century church father Eusebius, the story had a happy ending. He said that Jesus' disciple Thaddeus went to Abgar and healed him. Eusebius did not doubt that Jesus could write. He also said that in the archives of Edessa he had actually seen the correspondence between the two. It did not seem to bother Him that this writing from Jesus did not find its way into the New Testament.

THIS LETTER WAS COPIED MANY TIMES

Between the third and eighth century this purported letter of Jesus was inscribed on stone, papyri, and broken pieces of pottery. The letter was also written on amulets. Obviously many people assumed that it was authentic.

THE AUTHENTICITY OF THE LETTER IS DISPUTED

The letter was not accepted as authentic by all early church authorities. Jerome and Augustine, writing about seventy years after Eusebius, state that Jesus did not leave anything in writing.

Though most scholars have rejected the story as legendary, an explanation has to be given why Eusebius would have argued for its authenticity.

There is no apparent motive that he would have had for vouching for the story if he did believe it to be true.

Some modern scholars are giving this story a second look. At best, we can say that it is not impossible that Jesus could have written this letter.

SUMMARY TO QUESTION 31
DID JESUS WRITE ANYTHING?

While the four gospels contain the words of other people about Jesus, we know that He had the ability to both read and write. These abilities were demonstrated in the New Testament.

In a synagogue in Nazareth, we are told that Jesus opened the scroll of the prophet Isaiah and read from a chosen part. There is no indication whatsoever that He had trouble reading the text. Indeed, He found the part in the scroll, read it, and then re-rolled the scroll. The inference is that He did this with ease. Thus, we have every indication that Jesus had the ability to read.

We also know that Jesus Christ had the ability to write. In the story of the woman taken in adultery that is found in John's gospel, we are informed that Jesus wrote something on the ground that forced the religious leaders to leave Him and the woman alone. While we do not know exactly what He wrote, it was specific enough to cause the religious leaders to leave Him and the woman.

Though this portion of John's gospel is disputed because it is not found in the earliest manuscripts, almost everyone agrees that this is an actual event that took place in the life of Christ. We can thus conclude that Jesus could both read and write—though He did not leave us anything which has become part of Holy Scripture.

There is also an ancient tradition that Jesus actually wrote a letter to a king named Abgar. In response to Abgar's written request that Jesus visit him to bring him back to health, Jesus allegedly wrote back in return. From other sources we know that Abgar was an actual king who lived during the time of Christ. While it does not seem possible to confirm this story, there are a number of scholars who believe it did take place and that Jesus actually wrote something to this ancient king. All that we can know for certain is that Jesus could have written letters or books if He so wished.

Why Jesus Christ did not leave anything for us in writing, whether it be a systematic arrangement of His teachings, or His inner thoughts, we simply do not know. Because the Bible does not tell us why we do not have anything written from His hand, it is best not to speculate about why this is the case. Indeed, our job is to read and study the writings that He did leave us through His specially chosen representatives—the New Testament.

QUESTION 32

What About Alleged Sayings Of Jesus That Are Not Found In The Four Gospels? (Agrapha)

There are a number of alleged sayings of Jesus that exist that are not found in the four gospels. These are known as the "agrapha" (which means, "not written"). Some of them come relatively early in the history of the church. What should we make of these sayings? Do they accurately reflect the words of Jesus?

We can make the following observations about these sayings.

1. JESUS SPOKE MANY THINGS THAT ARE NOT RECORDED

To begin with, the New Testament itself says that Jesus did many things that have not been recorded in the four gospels. Indeed, John finished his gospel by saying the following.

> Now there are also many other things that Jesus did. Were every one of them to be written, I suppose that the world itself could not contain the books that would be written (John 21:25 ESV).

Therefore, numerous sayings and deeds of Jesus were never recorded. From what John wrote, it seems clear that there was a multitude of things which Jesus said and did which he could have chosen to write about. What we have in the four gospels is only a small portion of what could have been written.

2. THE WRITERS WERE SELECTIVE IN WHAT THEY RECORDED

This brings us to our next point. According to the New Testament itself, the writers were selective about what they wrote concerning Jesus.

We read the following in the gospel of John.

> Jesus performed many other miracles that his disciples saw. Those miracles are not written in this book. But these miracles have been written so that you will believe that Jesus is the Messiah, the Son of God, and so that you will have life by believing in him (John 20:30,31 God's Word).

This means that He said and did many more things than the four gospels record. The question then becomes, "Are any of those sayings or deeds found in other early writings?" "Have others recorded any words from Jesus which we do not find in the gospels?"

3. ONE SAYING OF JESUS NOT FOUND IN THE FOUR GOSPELS: (ACTS 20:35)

There is the issue of sayings of Jesus that are not found in the four gospels but they are recorded elsewhere in the New Testament. In fact, one saying of Jesus, not recorded in the four gospels, is found in the Book of Acts. We read the following.

> In all things I have shown you that by working hard in this way we must help the weak and remember the words of the Lord Jesus, how he himself said, 'It is more blessed to give than to receive' (Acts 20:35 ESV).

This particular saying of Jesus has not been recorded in the four gospels—yet we do find it in the New Testament.

4. MANY ALLEGED SAYINGS OF JESUS DO EXIST OUTSIDE OF THE NEW TESTAMENT

From sources outside of the four gospels there are a number of sayings that have claimed to come from Jesus. For example, the Gospel of Thomas contains 114 separate sayings that are introduced by the words, "Jesus said."

From other early sources, we find similar claims of recording authentic sayings of Jesus. Elaborate theories about Jesus have been built upon some of these sayings that are not found in the New Testament.

5. THERE IS NO CONSENSUS ABOUT WHICH SAYINGS ARE AUTHENTIC

While there are a number of Bible scholars who contend that we possess a number of statements from Jesus that are not recorded in the New Testament, there is no consensus on this issue. Some of the statements that are attributed to Jesus may indeed have come from Him, while others clearly do not reflect His character and teaching. For example, we find the following.

> Let Mary go away from us because women are not worthy of life.

This statement is certainly at odds with what we know of Jesus from the four gospels. Therefore, it is utterly rejected as coming from Him.

6. SOME POSSIBLE SAYINGS OF JESUS NOT FOUND IN THE NEW TESTAMENT

We can list a sample of sayings that some have argued were original with Jesus. They include the following.

In the margin of an ancient New Testament manuscript, Codex Bezae, we find the following reading in Luke 6:5.

> Man, if you know what you are doing you will be blessed; but if you do not know you are cursed and an offender of the law.

There are those who believe that Jesus actually did say this—or something similar.

There was a statement attributed to Jesus that is found in the writings of Clement of Alexandria which some argue may have been original with Jesus. It reads.

Be approved money changers.

It is possible that one or more of these sayings were actually uttered by Jesus. On the other hand, no one can be certain that Jesus spoke these things—or anything like it. All we can say that it is possible that Jesus said these things—or something similar.

7. WE CANNOT SAY FOR CERTAIN IF ANY SAYINGS ARE AUTHENTIC

Consequently we cannot be certain that we have any authentic saying of Jesus in the writings that are found outside of the New Testament. The best that can be done is to say that some of these sayings may have come from Jesus. We cannot go beyond that.

What we can say is this. The four gospel writers were either eyewitnesses to the life of Jesus Christ or they recorded eyewitness testimony. They certainly contain the authentic words of Jesus. The sources for these other sayings are unknown. We have to leave it at that. Indeed, we just do not know.

SUMMARY TO QUESTION 32
WHAT ABOUT ALLEGED SAYINGS OF JESUS THAT ARE NOT FOUND IN THE FOUR GOSPELS? (AGRAPHA)

From the New Testament itself, we know that Jesus Christ said and did many things that are not recorded in the Scriptures. Indeed, John ends his gospel by making reference to a multitude of things which Jesus said, and deeds which He did, that are not recorded in the New Testament. This makes it clear that the New Testament does not record everything about Him.

Indeed, we find that elsewhere John specifically stated that he wrote selectively about Jesus' words and deeds. John said that he had composed his gospel for the purpose of causing belief in the Lord. In stating this, John also noted that Jesus said many other things which he did not record in his gospel.

We know that at least one saying of Jesus exists outside of the four gospels, Acts 20:35. Paul quotes Jesus saying, "It is more blessed to give than to receive."

The fact that Jesus said and did many things which the New Testament has not recorded has caused Bible students to examine certain documents that claim to have other authentic words of Jesus. These sayings are known as the "agrapha," —unwritten sayings of Jesus.

Many of these alleged sayings exist. The problem is that there is no consensus as to which sayings, if any, actually came from Jesus. Since we cannot say for certain, it is unwise to build any theory about Jesus on these contested sayings.

What we do know for certain is that the New Testament contains the only undisputed sayings of Jesus. They were recorded by people who actually heard what He had said, or by people who wrote down the testimony of the eyewitnesses. It is from these documents that we go to discover what Jesus truly said.

QUESTION 33

What Are Some Of The Accounts Of Jesus That Differ From The New Testament? Could They Tell The Real Story?

Is the New Testament the only written document that contains reliable information about the words and deeds of Jesus? Are there other sources, apart from the gospels, that give us correct information about His life and ministry?

Some people think so. Throughout history, there have been a number of documents written that supposedly supplement what the four gospels tell us, or, in some cases, contradict what they say. Should we believe these documents rather than the four gospels?

We can divide these sources into two distinct groups: sources that are used by some modern scholars to reconstruct Jesus' words, and sources that nobody takes seriously but have become popular among the masses.

SOURCES USED BY SOME MODERN SCHOLARS

There are a number of sources that are variously used by modern scholars to reconstruct the life and ministry of Jesus. They include, but are not limited to, the following works.

1. THE GOSPEL OF THOMAS

The "Gospel of Thomas" was a document probably written in the second century A.D. It consists of a group of sayings purportedly made by Jesus. There is no historical context for these sayings. Some of them are identical, or similar, to the sayings of Jesus as found in the four gospels. Other sayings are completely different.

2. THE GOSPEL OF PETER

There is another ancient work called the "Gospel of Peter" that allegedly was written by the most prominent of the apostles. It is mentioned, but not cited, in several ancient works. Like many other writings, it gives a view of Jesus that was influenced by Gnosticism—those who sought "secret" knowledge.

3. THE GOSPEL OF THE HEBREWS

One ancient work, of which we only know about through other writings, is the "Gospel of the Hebrews." This work has not survived in any manuscript form. We only know about it from other writings.

4. THE SECRET GOSPEL OF MARK

The "Secret Gospel of Mark" was supposedly additions to Mark's Gospel that were later made by of Mark himself. No such document has been discovered—rather a copy of a manuscript reportedly written the second century churchman, Clement, cites what he claims are portions from this secret gospel. However, the manuscript that revealed the existence of the secret gospel of Mark is itself now gone.

5. THE CROSS GOSPEL

Some modern scholars give credence to a work known as the "Cross Gospel." Among other things, it describes a giant Jesus coming out of the tomb as well as a talking cross! While obviously legendary in content, some scholars see certain things in this work they believe to be earlier than the four gospels.

6. THE EGERTON PAPYRUS

The Egerton Papyrus is a small scrap of ancient papyrus that contains a few sayings that supposedly came from Jesus. Some scholars believe that these sayings may be authentic.

7. THE PROTEVANGELIUM OF JAMES

The "Protevangelium of James" is an ancient document that fills in some of the gaps in the life of Christ.

Not all scholars use each of these documents. Yet they have been variously used in an attempt to write the true story of Jesus.

POPULAR ACCOUNTS THAT NOBODY TAKES SERIOUSLY

There are a number of accounts about Jesus, His silent years, as well as events in His life that the gospels do not cover, that have been written about. Three of the most notable are the "Archko Volume," "The Aquarian Gospel of Jesus the Christ," and "The Lost Books of the Bible." We will briefly describe each of these here but devote an individual question to each where we go into further detail.

THE ARCHKO VOLUME

The "Archko Volume" has enjoyed popularity among for a number of years as an accurate account of certain aspects of the life of Christ which are not recorded in the New Testament. However, it is a fraud.

THE AQUARIAN GOSPEL OF JESUS THE CHRIST

There is a work known as, "The Aquarian Gospel of Jesus the Christ." It allegedly gives us information about Jesus' silent years. This work is also fraudulent.

THE LOST BOOKS OF THE BIBLE

The "Lost Books of the Bible" are a compilation of writings that claim to give early information about Jesus. However, they do no such thing.

A number of things need to be noted about these writings.

NOT ALL OF THESE WRITINGS ARE TAKEN SERIOUSLY BY SCHOLARS

These writings are the most celebrated among scholars and lay people. However, as we have indicated, not all of these writings have been taken seriously—even by unbelieving scholars. Works such as the Archko Volume, the Aquarian Gospel of Jesus the Christ, and the Lost Books of the Bible are obvious frauds written later in history. No one really believes they are what they claim to be. We only mention them because they have achieved some sort of popularity among the masses.

However, these other writings mentioned are believed by some scholars, to give an accurate alternative view of Jesus. This picture of Christ is different than the one found in the New Testament.

In fact, there are not any good reasons to accept the authenticity of these documents, and many good reasons to reject them. Yet, for some people, these writings contain the real story of who Jesus was, and what He said.

THE KEY ISSUE: WHAT IS OUR STARTING POINT TO DISCOVER THE GENUINE JESUS?

These works cited are often used to cast doubt on the New Testament portrayal of Jesus. It is argued that they, not the four gospels, tell us what really happened. Consequently, these documents are used as the starting point to reconstruct the real Jesus.

Therefore, one has to decide which sources will be used to determine the genuine Jesus. Will it be the four gospels which everyone agrees—were written earlier, by known associates of Jesus, which claim eyewitness testimony, claim to tell the exact truth, and give specific historical details, and that do indeed match known history?

Or are we to accept later writings—that give us no historical setting, that are written at unknown times, by unknown writers who have no connection with Jesus, and which portray a radically different Jesus than the One found in the New Testament?

Many choose these later writings. The reasons why this is done are varied. However, the one thing which those who choose the later writings have in common is that they reject the supernatural picture of Jesus as recorded in the New Testament. This assumption, or pre-supposition, guides their quest. Before the evidence is considered, it is determined that the supernatural Jesus did not exist. The world view of the New Testament is considered unscientific and mythical. Therefore, it is to be rejected.

With this as a starting point, they then examine the ancient references to Jesus. Those accounts which teach a supernatural Jesus are rejected out-of-hand—because they do not fit what these people have assumed to be the truth.

POINTS TO BE RECOGNIZED BY THOSE WHO CHOOSE THE LATER WRITINGS OVER THE GOSPELS

If one does choose to believe these sources over the four gospels, a number of points need to be understood.

1. THE OTHER SOURCES WERE ALL WRITTEN LATER

There is no doubt that all of the other sources we possess were written long after the time of Jesus. While it is possible they contain earlier, accurate information, it is also possible they do not. What we do know is that they were written during a time when fanciful stories about Jesus were being told. Of this, there is no doubt.

2. THE HISTORICAL REFERENCES ARE FEW IN THESE WORKS

Add to this, the historical references are few. For example, the Gospel of Thomas allegedly consists of sayings of Jesus without giving any historical setting. It is an anthology of things the Lord supposedly said.

However, when He said them, and where He said them, is not stated. Thus, the specific historical references in these other works are few in number.

3. THESE WRITINGS CONTRADICT EVERYTHING KNOWN ABOUT JESUS FROM OTHER SOURCES

It should be observed that the things written about Jesus, from these other documents, contradict everything else we know about Him. Not only do they contradict the New Testament and the writings of the early Christians, they also contradict the writings of non-believers!

Indeed, as we have discovered, those who rejected Jesus' claims provide the same general outline of who He claimed to be, as well as what He said. This was not the issue. It is not that they did not know about Jesus' claims, or misunderstood them. They simply, for whatever reason did not believe them.

However, they never denied that He made the claims or was alleged to have performed miracles.

4. NONE OF US IS IN A POSITION TO DENY THE SUPERNATURAL JESUS

This last point is the most crucial. None of us, no matter what our background or training, is in a position to rule out the possibility of a supernatural Jesus. Granted, this has not been our own personal experience. Indeed, we do not see the same sort of things today which are pictured in the New Testament.

However, this does not mean that they cannot occur, or never have occurred. In fact, the whole point of Jesus' coming to earth was to demonstrate His uniqueness. John's gospel notes the following about the words of Jesus.

> The temple guards answered, "No human has ever spoken like this man" (John 7:46 God's Word).

No one has ever spoken like Jesus, no one has ever done the sort of things Jesus did. Why is this so? The Bible says it is because Jesus Christ is the unique Son of God, the Second Person of the Holy Trinity.

Furthermore, the New Testament not only makes these claims about Jesus, it backs them up with convincing evidence. Consequently, it is the place where one should go to learn about the real Jesus!

SUMMARY TO QUESTION 33
WHAT ARE SOME OF THE ACCOUNTS OF JESUS THAT DIFFER FROM THE NEW TESTAMENT? COULD THEY TELL THE REAL STORY?

We find that there are a number of written accounts about Jesus, apart from the New Testament, that claim some sort of authority, or have had certain claims made for them. They can be divided into two general categories.

First, there are works which certain New Testament scholars assume contain authoritative words about Jesus. Yet there is another group of writings which have become popular with large groups of people which no scholar takes seriously.

A number of people argue that some of these writings give a more authentic picture of Jesus than the New Testament. They use these writings as their starting point in their search for the genuine Jesus. However, there is nothing in these documents that give us any reason to believe that they contain more trustworthy information about Jesus than the four gospels.

First, all of them were composed later than the gospels. They were written during the time when many fanciful stories about Jesus were circulating. This fact alone makes these writings suspect.

There is also the lack of specific historical references in these works. Contrast this to the four gospels—which provide us with many detailed references as to where Jesus was when He made certain statements, and when He performed certain miraculous deeds. However, these others writings contain no specific testimony as to where or when Jesus said these things which they attribute to Him.

A huge problem is that these works not only contradict the four gospels, they also contradict the secular sources about Jesus! In other words, they present a Jesus that nobody else wrote about. Neither friend nor foe knew of a Jesus that these documents write about.

Much of the motivation to use these writings, rather than the four gospels, is the desire to have a Jesus who is not a supernatural Jesus. They do not want to acknowledge the One who is the Savior of the world and eventually will be its Judge. Yet none of us are in a position to do this. Furthermore, when we examine the evidence we find that the New Testament portrayal of a supernatural Jesus is one which fits the facts.

What Is The Gospel Of Thomas?

There were numerous false Gospels, false Acts of the Apostles, false New Testament Letters and Apocalypses that circulated in the early church. One of the most important of these works is what is known as, "The Gospel of Thomas."

WHAT IS THE GOSPEL OF THOMAS?

In 1945, a 5th century manuscript was discovered that was written in ancient Coptic, or Egyptian. When translated, it was found to be an ancient text with a number of alleged sayings of Jesus. This document is known as the "Gospel of Thomas."

The Gospel of Thomas was probably originally composed in Greek about the year A.D. 140. It was likely written in the city of Edessa in Syria. It is dated at this time because some of the sayings found in it are parallel to those in the Oxyrhynchus papyri which can be dated around A.D.150,

Consisting of 114 sayings of Jesus, it is the most extensive collection of non-biblical sayings of Christ that still exist. A close examination reveals that about half of them have some correspondence to sayings of Jesus in the four Gospels. However, hardly any of them are exactly the same. Some of the sayings are similar to those known previously from the writings of the early Christians. About forty of these saying are entirely new—found nowhere else in history.

WHO IS THE ALLEGED AUTHOR THOMAS?

There is some confusion as to the identity of the writer of the Gospel of Thomas. Some believe that the alleged author is the Thomas that is known to us from the New Testament. This Thomas, who was one of Jesus' Twelve Disciples, is called Thomas, or, "the twin."

However, others believe the gospel of Thomas was supposedly written by another Thomas. He was the alleged twin brother of Jesus. Yet, Jesus had no "twin brother." The gospels make it very clear that He was the born without a twin.

THE CONTENT OF THE GOSPEL OF THOMAS

The Gospel of Thomas begins as follows.

> These are the secret words which the living Jesus spoke and Didymus Judas Thomas wrote. And he said: Whosoever finds the explanation of these words shall not taste death.

REASONS FOR REJECTING THE GOSPEL OF THOMAS

While many fanciful claims have been made for this work, we know that the Gospel of Thomas is unreliable for the following reasons.

1. THERE WAS A SECRET APPROACH TO THE MESSAGE OF JESUS

The secret approach found in the Gospel of Thomas is typical of the writings of the Gnostics—those who supposedly had "secret" knowledge. Although we should mention that there are some questions as to whether this work is a Gnostic writing.

Whatever the case may be, in contrast to the Gospel of Thomas, the four Gospels are open about the ways of salvation and the kingdom of God. Indeed, Jesus talked about proclaiming the truth openly to everyone. We read the following words of our Lord in Matthew.

What I tell you in the dark, speak in the daylight; what is whispered in your ear, proclaim from the roofs (Matthew 10:27 NIV).

The differences between what Jesus said, and the emphasis on secrecy which we find in the Gospel of Thomas, could not be greater. In sum, the Gospel of Thomas contains "secret" sayings while the four gospels make it clear that Jesus' message is to be heard by everyone everywhere in the most public of manners.

Indeed, in front of the former High Priest, Annas, Jesus made it clear that His was an open message to the world. He said.

Jesus answered him, "I spoke openly to the world. I always taught in synagogues and in the temple, where the Jews always meet, and in secret I have said nothing" (John 18:20 NKJV).

Secrecy was contrary to the public nature of Jesus' teachings. It was not His custom to teach only "secret truths" to His disciples.

2. THERE IS NO HISTORICAL SETTING FOR THE SAYINGS

Another problem is that there is no historical setting for the statements. The Gospel of Thomas is a compilation of sayings without the inclusion of important historical events—as those recorded in the four gospels. We are not told when, or under what circumstances, any of these statements were made.

In contrast, the gospels always place Jesus' words in historical contexts. There is an authentic setting where He gave His teachings. There is none in the Gospel of Thomas.

3. THE TEACHING OFTEN CONTRADICTS THE FOUR GOSPELS

Many of the sayings found in the Gospel of Thomas are contradictory to those we have in the Gospels. For example, saying 114 says.

Jesus said, 'See, I shall lead her, so that I will make her male, that she too many become a living spirit, resembling you males. For every woman who makes herself male will enter the Kingdom of Heaven.'

This is an absurd idea. According to this supposed statement of Jesus, a female has to first become a male before entering the kingdom of God! Nothing like this is even remotely taught by Jesus—or anywhere else in the Bible for that matter.

4. IT PRESENTS A DIFFERENT JESUS

In the Gospel of Thomas, the Person of Jesus Christ is different than the One revealed in the four Gospels. In the Gospels, Jesus is God the Son, Second Person of the Holy Trinity. He is God Himself who became a human being in order to let us know what God is like.

Yet in the Gospel of Thomas, Jesus is one who points the way by which an individual can attain the knowledge of God. Again, the contrast could not be greater.

The Scripture also warns believers about false portrayals of Jesus like the one we find in the Gospel of Thomas. Paul wrote.

> I am astonished that you are so quickly deserting him who called you in the grace of Christ and are turning to a different gospel—not that there is another one, but there are some who trouble you and want to distort the gospel of Christ. But even if we or an angel from heaven should preach to you a gospel contrary to the one we preached to you, let him be accursed (Galatians 1:6-8 ESV).

This is not merely an academic issue. Notice that Paul says that anyone who proclaims a different message about Jesus, than the one we find in the New Testament, is placed under a divine curse!

He also warned the Corinthians about those which proclaim "another Jesus."

> For if a person comes and preaches another Jesus, whom we did not preach, or you receive a different spirit, which you had not received, or a different gospel, which you had not accepted, you put up with it splendidly (2 Corinthians 11:4 HCSB).

These reasons, along with many others, demonstrate that the Gospel of Thomas is a forgery—rather than a legitimate work written by one of Jesus' apostles or confidants. It is representative of other forgeries that were circulated at that time.

5. THOMAS IS ASSUMED TO BE THE BEST SOURCE OF JESUS' LIFE BY SOME

Unhappily, a small group of fringe scholars has claimed that the Gospel of Thomas is actually a more accurate, trustworthy record of what Jesus said than what we have in the four gospels. Although written about one hundred years after Jesus' death and resurrection, and only listing a number of sayings, it is claimed to be "the source" where we should derive our portrait of Jesus. This approach certainly does not fit the evidence.

There is something else which we must take into consideration. Independent studies of the Gospel of Thomas seem to show that the writer of this document knew the Gospels as they now stand. He did not have, as some contend, an earlier written source of Jesus' sayings that were composed before the four gospels.

In sum, the Gospel of Thomas is not the place where we should go to determine what Jesus said, or did not say. The only place to discover the truth is with the four gospels. They alone contain the authoritative words and deeds of Jesus.

SUMMARY TO QUESTION 34
WHAT IS THE GOSPEL OF THOMAS?

After the New Testament period, there were a number of works that arose that claimed to have been written by someone who was mentioned in the New Testament. However, the works are nothing but forgeries. Among other things, these forgeries are known as the New Testament Pseudepigrapha. There are a number of gospels, acts, letters, and apocalypses that use the name of a biblical character as its author. Yet that person did not write the particular work that has his or her name on it.

One of the most prominent of these forgeries is the Gospel of Thomas. This work supposedly consists of a number of secret sayings of Jesus that are recorded by the disciple Thomas. Yet there is no evidence whatsoever of their authenticity.

On the contrary, the Gospel of Thomas fails for a number of reasons.

First, the approach is secret rather than the open approach of the gospels. Jesus emphasized that those who follow Him should publicly proclaim His teachings. The Gospel of Thomas, on the other hand, speaks of "secret" knowledge about Jesus. The contrast could not be greater.

In addition, there is no historical setting for these supposed sayings of Jesus. They are merely a group of sayings with no context to them. We do not know when or where Jesus supposedly said them. Contrast this to the gospels, where the sayings of Jesus are always placed in some historical context.

There is also the problem that many of the teachings of the Gospel of Thomas actually contradict the four gospels. Some of these teachings are truly absurd. They contain nothing like what we have in the New Testament.

Finally, the Gospel of Thomas presents a different Jesus than the one revealed in the New Testament. Scripture warns us ahead of time of those who present another Jesus—a Jesus which did not exist. This is what we have in the Gospel of Thomas.

Unhappily, there are some people who assume Thomas is the best source that we now have available to know what Jesus really said. However, there is no real reason to assume this is the case. The evidence seems to show that Thomas knew the four gospels as they now stand and simply rearranged a number of the sayings of Jesus. There is no evidence whatsoever that would cause us to believe he had some source that predated the gospels. Consequently, the Gospel of Thomas is worthless in giving us a true portrait of Jesus. For this, we must go to the four gospels.

What Is The Secret Gospel Of Mark?

In 1958, an ancient manuscript came to light that spoke of a previously unknown work called, the "Secret Gospel of Mark" or "Secret Mark." It has been claimed that this ancient text actually cites material that was left out of the Gospel of Mark when first written but was later added by Mark himself.

THE ALLEGED DISCOVERY

This alleged discovery was supposedly made in the library of a monastery located in the Judean desert in Israel called Mar Saba. It consists of a previous unknown letter from Clement of Alexandria, a second century church figure, who wrote to a previously unknown person called Theodore.

This letter contained references to a previously unknown work called the "Secret Gospel of Mark." The manuscript of this letter was written in Greek, most likely in the eighteenth century. Supposedly, it was attached to a seventeenth century copy of the letters of another church father, Ignatius.

THE CLAIM: MARK ADDED LATER ELEMENTS TO HIS GOSPEL

According to this letter from Clement, Mark left out certain things in his written gospel. When he left Rome and arrived in Alexandria,

Egypt, he then added these "secret matters." These later truths would lead the readers, or hearers, into some sort of deeper spiritual understanding. This secret gospel was carefully guarded and read only by those who had been initiated into the "great mysteries."

This letter of Clement goes on to say that a man named Carpocrates had acquired a copy of "secret Mark" and was using it to support his false teaching. He was distorting what secret Mark actually said. Thus, Clement, quotes the exact text of "secret Mark" to allow the person to whom he was writing to respond to the false use of this secret work.

PROBLEMS WITH SECRET MARK

There are a number of problems with the work from Clement that informs us of the existence of "Secret Mark."

THE MANUSCRIPT MYSTERIOUSLY DISAPPEARED

For one thing, the manuscript has mysteriously disappeared. There is some question as to whether anyone, apart from the scholar who supposedly discovered it, ever saw it. All that is left are photographs of the manuscript. Consequently, no independent evaluation of this manuscript has ever been made. This is a major problem.

THE MANUSCRIPT COPY SEEMS TOO GOOD

There are further problems. Some scholars find this eighteenth century copy of this letter too good—a spotless copy of an ancient text. The fact that it mysteriously disappeared also gives cause for concern.

IT LOOKS LIKE SOMEONE IS TRYING TO SOUND LIKE MARK

In addition, the quotations from "Secret Mark" sound too much like Mark to actually be the New Testament Mark. It is though someone is trying very hard to sound like Mark. In other words, it is the work of a twentieth century forger. That such a letter from Clement ever existed is also doubted.

SOME SCHOLARS BELIEVE CLEMENT MAY HAVE WRITTEN THIS LETTER

However, there are some scholars who do believe that we do have an actual copy of a correspondence by Clement. If this is what it actually turns out to be, then it would be similar to many other mid-second century Gnostic writings. The writer to whom it was attributed, Clement, was quite a gullible individual whose writings contain other references to Gnostic texts. In any case, this document would be worthless to use as a source of information to determine the real historical Jesus.

MARK COMPILED PETER'S RECOLLECTIONS OF JESUS

There are a number of important points to make. For one thing, the evidence leads us to believe Mark only recorded the words of the Apostle Peter. That is, he put together into writing a number of messages that Peter spoke to an audience while they were in Rome.

Therefore, Mark should not be called the writer of his gospel in the traditional understanding of the term writer. He was more of a compiler. This being the case, it is hard to imagine that he would add his own thoughts to a work which was really not his.

In sum, what we have today is a non-existent manuscript of a "secret" work which no other source in history tells us ever existed and that no scholar has independently verified. Yet, as can probably be imagined, a number of people not only take this questionable work seriously, they use it as the basis to determine the identity of the "real Jesus." From "Secret Mark," Jesus turns out to be a magician as well as someone who has morally questionable practices.

Though there is no objective reason as to why anyone should use this document to reconstruct the genuine Jesus, we are not always dealing with objectivity when the issue of Jesus' identity arises. People will always want to use sources such as "Secret Mark" in a futile attempt to find a different Jesus—as well as to remove any personable responsibility they may have toward Him.

However, this will not work. According to Scripture, there will come a day when everyone must stand before Jesus and give an account for their belief, or non-belief, in Him. This includes those who advocate this worthless document "secret Mark."

SUMMARY TO QUESTION 35
WHAT IS THE SECRET GOSPEL OF MARK?

In 1958, an ancient letter, supposedly written by the second century Christian Clement of Alexandria, cites a portion of what is known as the "Secret Gospel of Mark." This "Secret Mark" has been alleged to contain additions to Mark's gospel. To many, Mark is the earliest source for the life of Jesus. These additions are claimed to have been made by Mark himself when he was in Alexandria, Egypt. This would make this manuscript extremely important for gospel study.

Yet there is no evidence whatsoever that this is the case. Indeed, there would be no reason for Mark to add any secret material to his gospel seeing that he was basically a stenographer, or recorder, of a number of sermons given by Peter. Mark, therefore, is not a writer in the traditional sense but rather a compiler of the sermons of the Apostle Peter.

This being the case, it is hard to imagine how Mark would assume that he had authority to add to what the leader of the apostles taught about Jesus. Especially since the material in "secret Mark" contradicts the main elements of the Gospel that bears his name!

Furthermore, "Secret Mark" may be nothing more than a twentieth century forgery. Indeed, there are too many suspicious things surrounding its discovery, as well as its unexplained disappearance before anyone had a chance to independently verify its truthfulness.

Whatever the case may be, to give priority to a document that no one has seen, and which has never been subjected to any independent verification, is neither a reasonable nor a scholarly thing to do.

Yet for people who attempt to escape the responsibility of answering to a Holy God, this "secret" Mark gives them the excuse they need. Unfortunately, believing this is the genuine account of Jesus' words and deeds will not help them at all come Judgment Day.

What Is The Aquarian Gospel Of Jesus Christ?

Throughout the history of the church many documents have surfaced that have claimed to have been written by the Apostles, or those intimately familiar with the life of Jesus Christ. A number of these works have surfaced in the last few hundred years. Because they have gained some sort of popularity they must be addressed. One of the most prominent is known as "The Aquarian Gospel of Jesus the Christ."

THE AQUARIAN GOSPEL OF JESUS THE CHRIST

The Aquarian Gospel of Jesus the Christ was written by a Civil War chaplain named Levi H. Dowling (1844-1911). It was based upon alleged communication he received from a "universal mind." The Aquarian Gospel attempts to fill in some of the missing years of Jesus' youth, as well as explain His wisdom by attributing it to contact with holy men of other religions. The result is a contradictory mixture of Christian Science and occultic thought.

The name is derived from the astrological idea that a new Aquarian age has come upon us, bringing with it the need for a new spiritual gospel— the Aquarian gospel.

THE CONTENT OF THE AQUARIAN GOSPEL

The Aquarian Gospel of Jesus the Christ attempts to fill in some of the blanks in the life of Jesus. Some of the material in the Aquarian Gospel is borrowed from the ancient Gospel of James—a well-known forgery in the early years of the church. The most prominent part of the book deals with the education and travel of Jesus.

According to the Aquarian Gospel, Jesus first studied under the Jewish teacher Hillel and then went to India to spend time with their holy men— the Brahmins and Buddhists. His learning experience also supposedly took Him to Tibet, Persia, Assyria, Greece, and Egypt.

According to the Aquarian gospel, it was in Egypt that Jesus was said to have joined the sacred brotherhood. He passed through seven degrees, and emerged as the "Logos." In Alexandria, Egypt, a council of seven sages was held where they formulated seven great religious postulates and ordained Jesus for the work of the ministry.

The Aquarian Gospel rewrites the four gospels according to its own particular viewpoint. The end of the story has Jesus appearing in a materialized body to people in India, Persia, Greece, and other countries.

Dowling claimed to have received this information about Jesus from Akasha—which he alleged was an immense spiritual field that surrounds the earth. In the Aquarian Gospel, Jesus is not the unique Savior, or Son of God. He is merely the prototype of what every human being can be, the Christ.

EVALUATION OF THE AQUARIAN GOSPEL

Like many previous attempts, the Aquarian Gospel attempts to give an explanation of the wisdom and character of Jesus apart from the biblical depiction. Dowling's reconstruction shows obvious borrowing from the ancient "Gospel of James," as well as familiarity with a nineteenth century work, Novotitch's "Unknown Life of Jesus Christ."

The book begins with an historical inaccuracy: It reads, "Augustus Caesar reigned and Herod Antipas was ruler in Jerusalem." This is an historical error. Herod Antipas ruled in Galilee, never in Jerusalem. Thus the fraudulent nature of this work is evident from the beginning.

THE SOURCE OF JESUS' TEACHINGS

A crucial problem with the Aquarian Gospel concerns its idea as to the source of Jesus' teachings. If Jesus obtained His wisdom from the masters of India, Greece, and other countries, then why doesn't His teaching reflect it?

The teachings of Jesus, as recorded in the four Gospels, are in direct conflict with every central belief of Hinduism, Buddhism, and the other religions with which He supposedly came into contact!

IT GIVES A FALSE PORTRAIT OF JESUS

The simple fact is this: we have in the four Gospels a first-hand account of the life and ministry of Jesus. The Aquarian Gospel is a false portrait of the life of Christ. It is not based upon any historical records or eye-witness testimony, but rather upon the recollections of an ancient forgery and the imagination of a nineteenth-century writer. In the Aquarian gospel, Jesus is a master magician who believed in reincarnation. It has no value whatsoever in providing new or accurate information on the life of Christ. Consequently, it should not be taken seriously.

SUMMARY TO QUESTION 36
WHAT IS THE AQUARIAN GOSPEL OF JESUS THE CHRIST?

The Aquarian Gospel of Jesus the Christ was written by Civil War chaplain Levi Dowling to give a picture of the "real" Jesus. Like so many other writings of its kind, it is historically worthless.

This nineteenth century work attempts to fill in Jesus' missing years, as well as explain where He obtained His great wisdom. It has Jesus traveling to different lands to gain wisdom from certain "holy men." Upon His return, He imparted that newly gained wisdom to the people of Israel. The end result is a Jesus who is a prototype of what all of us can become—the Christ. This insightful truth about Jesus was supposed communicated to Levi Dowling by some spiritual force field which surrounds the earth.

While there have been those in the general public who have believed this work to be genuine, there is no historical basis whatsoever for it. While no scholar takes this work seriously, it has been used by certain "new age" groups to promote the idea that Jesus discovered truth about Himself that we also can discover about ourselves.

Like all other such works, it gives a false portrait of Jesus Christ while robbing Him of His unique identity. Indeed, the Bible says that Jesus is God the Son, the Second Person of the Holy Trinity. He became a human being to show us what the one true God is like. Thus, Jesus is unlike anyone who has ever lived, or ever will live.

Furthermore, we can indeed become God's children. This happens by placing our faith in Him. However, none of us will become "the Christ." He alone has that honor.

What Is
Archko Volume?

One of the most famous of the written hoaxes is the "Archko Volume." The work is also known as the "Report of Pilate" or "The Archko Library." The content of this work is an alleged report of the trial and death of Jesus made by Pontius Pilate to the Emperor Tiberius.

The existence of this work can be traced back to a certain Reverend W.D. Mahan from Boonville, Missouri. In 1879, he published a thirty-two-page pamphlet titled, "A Correct Transcript of Pilate's Court."

MORE DISCOVERIES WERE MADE BY MAHAN

The success of the "Report of Pilate" led Mahan to make some more "discoveries." These discoveries included an interview with the shepherds who were given the announcement of Christ's birth. There is also an interview with Joseph and Mary by the famous Jewish teacher Gamaliel. Found also is Eli's story of the Magi, and other previously unknown interviews surrounding the life and ministry of Jesus. Mahan claimed these "interviews" were translated from ancient manuscripts in Rome, or Constantinople.

THE WORK CONTAINS MANY HISTORICAL ERRORS

These other interviews are filled with historical errors. For example, he gives a number of references to Josephus's Jewish Wars that simply do not exist.

In addition, there is the false statement that Josephus in his Antiquities refers to Jesus in more than fifty places. This work also says that Tacitus wrote the biography of Agricola, his father in law, in the year A.D. 56. This is impossible since Tacitus was born in A.D. 55. Furthermore, there was no biography to write since Agricola was only nineteen at the time!

THE FRAUD IS EXPOSED

The so-called "Report of Pilate," as well as all of these later interviews were immediately exposed as the frauds that they clearly are. Unhappily, people continue to read and believe these fraudulent works although they have no basis in fact.

To discover who Jesus Christ truly is, one need only to pick up a New Testament and start reading! This will give us the true portrait of Him as well as the circumstances around His life and ministry. The Archko Volume provides no help whatsoever.

SUMMARY TO QUESTION 37
WHAT IS THE ARCHKO VOLUME?

The Archko Volume claims to contain some amazing information surrounding the life and times of Jesus Christ. This includes a series of "interviews" with key New Testament figure. It began with a transcript of the interview Pontius Pilate had with Jesus as He was being put on trial for His life. Other "interviews" were soon discovered after this one. They include an interview with the shepherds who were given the announcement of the birth of Christ by the angel of the Lord! We are told of their thoughts and feelings. An interview of Jesus' earthly parents, Joseph and Mary, was also discovered.

It would indeed be something special if we had the transcript of Jesus' interview with Pilate, the thoughts of those first shepherds who heard the announcement of Jesus' birth, as well as the feelings of Joseph and Mary. However, the Archko Volume does not provide us with an accurate account of events in the first century as it claims to be. Rather, it is a poorly written hoax that dated from the nineteenth century by a certain Reverend W.D. Mahan. Consequently, it is of no help whatsoever in adding to our knowledge of Jesus, His disciples, or the world into which Jesus came.

Unfortunately, it continues to be published and read as though it gives the public some trustworthy information about Jesus Christ. Yet it is historically worthless. Again we emphasize—the only accurate first-hand account of Jesus' life and ministry is found in the New Testament.

While we may wish to have more information about what happened when Jesus stood before Pilate, as well as the thoughts of those shepherds who received the announcement of Christ's birth, and the feelings of Joseph and Mary about their Son, this information is not available to us. The Archko Volume certainly does not help fill in the blanks.

QUESTION 38

What Are The Lost Books Of The Bible?

One of the most often-asked questions, about sources for the life of Jesus outside of the New Testament, concerns the so-called "Lost Books of the Bible." A book with this title was produced in 1926.

However, it was the reprint of William Hone's Apocryphal New Testament, first printed in 1820. Hone's book was copied from two earlier works which were published in 1736 and 1737. Thus, the materials found in the "Lost Books of the Bible" were written over two hundred and eighty years ago. Since the time of the original writing of the lost books, the field of manuscript studies has made tremendous advances but those who publish these works have taken none of this into account.

The contents of the "lost books" include the following:

THE FOUR INFANCY GOSPELS

The Four Infancy Gospels include a work called, "The Birth of Mary," a work written in the middle of the second century; "The Protoevangelium of James," written about the same time; the "First Gospel of Infancy," composed about A.D. 400; and "The Second Infancy Gospel," which in reality is a fragment of the Gospel of Thomas.

These were so-called infancy gospels were written to fill in the details of the early years of the life of Christ of which we have no written record. These works include stories of Jesus forming clay figures of animals and birds, which He makes to walk, fly, and eat.

There is another account of a child who runs into Jesus and then the child falls down dead. These examples are representative of the fanciful nature of the accounts.

OTHER WORKS AMONG THE LOST BOOKS

There is also a work known as "The Acts of Pilate" which was written in the fourth or fifth century. Other works found among the lost books include the Apostles' Creed and the spurious letter from Paul to the Laodiceans.

As mentioned, these are not "lost books of the Bible." They are merely fictitious accounts of the life of Jesus and other characters mentioned in the New Testament. They are historically worthless.

Again we have repeatedly stated, it is only the New Testament which gives us the true words of Jesus. Therefore, it is to it alone which we must give our attention. It is better these "Lost Books of the Bible" remain lost as far as the reading public is concerned.

SUMMARY TO QUESTION 38
WHAT ARE THE LOST BOOKS OF THE BIBLE?

One popular work that purports to give us further information about the life and ministry of Jesus Christ is known as "The Lost Books of the Bible." As the title indicates, this is actually a collection of writings that claim to have authority similar to that of Holy Scripture. Among their contents are the "four infancy gospels."

These works attempt to fill in some of the details about Jesus' early years that the New Testament omits. Indeed, a number of personal stories about the youthful Jesus are given to us in these works.

While this is indeed an intriguing title, the lost books of the Bible are not really "lost." Instead, they are a collection of unhistorical ancient writings that make a worthless attempt to fill in some of the details of the life of Jesus. They are part of a long list of writings that came centuries after the time of Christ. These writings have no historical basis whatsoever.

These works, like so many others, attempt to fill in the gaps in Jesus' life and ministry that are not recorded for us in the New Testament. Because people are naturally curious about Jesus' silent years, writings that claimed to give accurate details were read and circulated.

However, those in authority in the church realized their worthlessness. Consequently they were never considered of any worth because they do not add to our knowledge of Jesus and His life and times.

It is important that works like these be ignored for they are a waste of time to read. To discover the "real" Jesus is simple. One must simply open up the Bible and start reading the New Testament. This will provide the reader with an accurate firsthand account of who Jesus is, as well as what He truly did.

QUESTION 39

What Should We Conclude About The Various Written Accounts Of Jesus Christ?

There is no doubt that Jesus Christ existed. Both friend and foe testify to this. Having looked at the evidence that we have about the life and ministry of Jesus from ancient written sources, we can make the following observations about them.

To begin with, the writings we have about Jesus can be placed into two categories. The authentic information can be found in the New Testament, particularly the four gospels. All other written sources, whether ancient or modern, are of no help whatsoever, in determining what Jesus said and did.

THE FOUR GOSPELS ARE THE ONLY TRUSTWORTHY SOURCE ABOUT JESUS

The four gospels are our only firsthand information that we presently have about the life and ministry of Jesus Christ. We know this to be a fact for at least the following five reasons. They are as follows.

1. THE TEXT HAS BEEN RELIABLY TRANSMITTED TO US

First, the text has been reliably transmitted to us. That is, it says the same thing today as when originally written. Consequently we have the confidence that we are reading the exact same words which the writers originally penned. Nothing has been added or subtracted.

2. THE WRITERS INTENDED TO GIVE US AN ACCURATE ACCOUNT OF JESUS

Second, the gospel writers intended to give us an accurate portrait of the life and ministry of Jesus. Their desire was to tell the truth about Him. It was their stated goal to give us the "exact truth" about what Jesus said and did.

3. THEY WERE IN A POSITION TO GIVE US AN ACCURATE ACCOUNT OF JESUS

Third, these writers were in a position to give humanity a correct understanding of what Jesus said and did. They were there when the events took place. These disciples heard what Jesus taught, as well as seeing the things which He did.

4. THEIR PICTURE OF JESUS AND HIS TIMES IS HISTORICALLY ACCURATE

Fourth, the evidence shows they did exactly that. From all available sources, we can conclude that their picture of Jesus matches with known reality. Indeed, what these people wrote matches up with the known laws, customs, people and events of the first century A.D.

5. ALL OTHER WRITINGS ABOUT JESUS CHRIST COME LATER IN TIME

Finally, all other writings that claim to contain trustworthy information about Jesus are not firsthand sources of His life and ministry. They can add nothing whatsoever to our knowledge of what He said and did. This brings us to our next point.

OTHER WRITINGS ABOUT JESUS ARE NOT OUTLAW SCRIPTURES

There are a number of conclusions that we can make about certain writings contain information about the life of Jesus that have not made it into the New Testament.

Some ill-informed people have called these books "outlaw" Scriptures. But this is certainly not the case. Indeed, none of these works were ever thought of as part of the New Testament. Anyone who insists that the early church suppressed these particular works, to keep the people from knowing the truth about Jesus, is speaking out of ignorance, or a desire to deceive. Several points need to be made.

1. THEY WERE WRITTEN AT A LATER DATE THAN THE BOOKS OF SCRIPTURE

It is obvious from the date of the composition of these works that they cannot be considered on the same level as Holy Scripture. The four gospels were written by eyewitnesses, or people who recorded eyewitness testimony of the life and ministry of Jesus. They were composed by people who were in a position to make authoritative statements of what Jesus said and did.

These other works were written by individuals who were in no such position to make authoritative statements about Jesus. They can add nothing to our knowledge of Him or His times because they were not there!

Thus, we have the clear contrast between the eyewitness account, the New Testament, and these other written works which were penned by people who were not living at Jesus' time.

2. THEY ARE NOT SECRET WORKS

There is something else which needs to be emphasized. These other writings cannot be called "secret works." Scholars have always been aware of these works. Indeed, they are not secret and have never been secret. One of the reasons why the general public has not heard of them is because no one takes them seriously. And for good reason!

3. THEY ARE REJECTED BY ALL BRANCHES OF CHRISTENDOM

Furthermore, all branches of Christianity reject these writings as giving us some type of authoritative understanding of the life and times of Jesus Christ. Indeed, Roman Catholics, the Orthodox Church, and

Protestants alike are in agreement that these writings have no place in Holy Scripture and do not add to our historical knowledge of Jesus.

4. THEY WERE NEVER CONSIDERED TO BE SCRIPTURE

In addition, these books have never received the slightest consideration as being part of the New Testament canon of Scripture. They are not in the category of some writings which were accepted by some but disputed by others. All believers rejected these books.

5. THE DIFFERENCES BECOME CLEAR IF ONE MERELY READS THEM

A reading of these written works will immediately demonstrate their inferior nature. There is simply no comparison between them and the writings that are found in Scripture. The fanciful nature becomes evident when the New Testament is read alongside these other writings.

6. THE SUPERIORITY OF THE NEW TESTAMENT IS CONFIRMED

Every other source that gives us a different understanding of Jesus, than the picture found in the New Testament, is discovered to be deficient. By examining these writings, and the claims made for them, we discover the superiority and the accuracy of the New Testament.

Thus, rather than taking away from our confidence in the four gospels, examining these other sources actually adds to our confidence. The vast difference between the four canonical gospels and all the other attempts to write about the life and times of Jesus Christ becomes clearer and clearer. There really is no comparison between them.

7. WE SHOULD LET THE NEW TESTAMENT SPEAK FOR ITSELF

This brings us to our final point. Since the New Testament is the only reliable source for the life and ministry of Jesus, we should let it speak to us. It should be our sole guide to determine who Jesus is, what He said and did, and what our responsibility is toward Him. We need to read it, study it, and let it tell us the truth about Jesus. This is how we can discover the "real" Jesus.

SUMMARY TO QUESTION 39
WHAT SHOULD WE CONCLUDE ABOUT THE VARIOUS WRITTEN ACCOUNTS OF JESUS CHRIST?

It is essential that have the correct idea of who Jesus Christ is as well as what He demands of us. Consequently, it is of the utmost importance that we have the proper sources to determine these things. After looking at the evidence, there are a number of conclusions we can make about various accounts of the life and times of Jesus Christ which have come down to us.

To begin with, the only reliable firsthand information that we have about the life and ministry of Jesus Christ comes from the New Testament. No other source is trustworthy.

For one thing, the text of the New Testament has been accurately transmitted to us. It says the same thing as when originally written. Moreover, these writers claim that they are attempting to provide us with a genuine portrait of Jesus. Add to this they were certainly in a position to do this—seeing that they were eyewitnesses of the events or recorded the testimony of eyewitnesses.

Furthermore, all the evidence shows that they did give us a trustworthy account of what Jesus said and did. Indeed, we discover that what they wrote, accurately matches up with what we know about the people, places, events, and customs of Jesus' time.

Finally, there is no other written source which has any claim to give us a more accurate picture of who Jesus was, or what He did. None whatsoever.

These other writings can lay no claim to being Holy Scripture. Nobody in the church ever considered these works to have any authoritative status. They are not "outlaw Scriptures." Indeed all branches of Christendom reject the idea that these writings have any authoritative status.

Furthermore, they are not "secret" writings. The believers have always known about them. They considered them to be historically worthless because they are historically worthless!

In sum, every other writing, apart from the New Testament, that attempts to fill in the gaps of the life of Jesus Christ, or to tell us different story, only reveals the superiority of the four Gospels.

To this day, there is no convincing evidence whatsoever that any of these or other writings give us first-hand material about Jesus. This being the case, if we want to know what Jesus truly said and did, we should listen to what the New Testament says about His identity, as well as the purpose of His coming to the earth. It alone gives us the genuine story.

About the Author

Don Stewart is a graduate of Biola University and Talbot Theological Seminary (with the highest honors).

Don is a best-selling and award-winning author having authored, or co-authored, over seventy books. This includes the best-selling *Answers to Tough Questions*, with Josh McDowell, as well as the award-winning book *Family Handbook of Christian Knowledge: The Bible*. His various writings have been translated into over thirty different languages and have sold over a million copies.

Don has traveled around the world proclaiming and defending the historic Christian faith. He has also taught both Hebrew and Greek at the undergraduate level and Greek at the graduate level.

Made in the USA
San Bernardino, CA
08 November 2016